Thirsty,

Swimming in

the Lake

Thirsty, Swimming in the Lake

the Lake

Essentials of Constructive Living

David K. Reynolds, Ph.D.

Quill
William Morrow
New York

Copyright © 1991 by David K. Reynolds, Ph.D.

All rights reserved. No part of this book may be reproduced or utilized in any
form or by any means, electronic or mechanical, including photocopying, re-
cording, or by any information storage or retrieval system, without permission in
writing from the Publisher. Inquiries should be addressed to Permissions Department, William Morrow and Company, Inc., 1350 Avenue of the Americas, New
York, N.Y. 10019.

It is the policy of William Morrow and Company, Inc., and its imprints and affiliates,
recognizing the importance of preserving what has been written, to print the books
we publish on acid-free paper, and we exert our best efforts to that end.

The Library of Congress has catalogued the hardcover as follows:

Reynolds, David K.
    Thirsty, swimming in the lake / David K. Reynolds
        p.   cm.
    Includes bibliographical references.
    ISBN 0-688-11032-0(pbk.)
    1. Morita psychotherapy. 2. Naikan psychotherapy. I. Title.
RC489.M65R45   1991
616.89'14—dc20   91-6730
                                                                          CIP

Printed in the United States of America

First Quill Edition

1 2 3 4 5 6 7 8 9 10

BOOK DESIGN BY LISA STOKES

In memory of Ishin Yoshimoto,
founder of Naikan

Acknowledgments

My research in Japan was funded, in part, by the Mental Health Okamoto Memorial Foundation.

My colleagues in the constructive-living movement continue to teach me with their words and their lives. And the hundreds of readers who kindly wrote encouragement and suggestions and personal confirmation of the effectiveness of these methods have provided inspiration during the sometimes tedious writing process.

Contents

Introduction

Constructive living is a development and extension of ideas from Japan and other countries. The two major Japanese streams of thought in constructive living are called Morita therapy and Naikan. In this book when I identify something as Moritist, it comes directly from the writings of Morita Masatake or his followers. Similarly, Naikan elements of constructive living come from the writings of Yoshimoto Ishin and his followers. When I identify a constructive-living principle or practice, I mean that either the ideas came from Moritist or Naikan thought and I cannot recall direct teachings on the subject or that the ideas were developed outside of Japan.

This constructive living is not new age. It is closer to old hat. Perhaps you know the Zen tale about a man who comes for guidance from a Zen master but won't accept the advice he receives. The master pours the guest's cup full of tea and keeps on pouring. It overflows. When a cup is already full, you cannot pour more into it. Too many of the people I see these days want a constant trickle into their cups to make sure it stays right to the brim. They don't want to empty those cups of their familiar, though tepid, contents. Some students are what I call couch-wise. They have tried various psychotherapies. They have some sophistication about what can and what cannot be delivered in therapy. Nevertheless, they expect to sit and talk about their feelings hour after hour. Constructive living takes these people by surprise.

Constructive living makes no undelivered promises. It works to help students control what is controllable in human life. It is a modest but effective method for dealing with human misery.

Since I have more than twenty books in print, people may think of me as a prolific writer, but I simply write the same truth over and over—now in caps, now in small letters, now in gothic, now in roman, now in printing, now in script. How simple are these truths! And how varied they are in their forms!

" 'Not knowing how close the Truth is to them,
Beings seek for it afar—what a pity!
It is like those who being in water
Cry out for water, feeling thirst.' "

—Shibayama, Zenkei, *A Flower Does Not Talk*

MINDING THE MIND

In this section are presented an assortment of constructive-living issues and information. Intellectual understanding of the principles of constructive living may be helpful, but the experiential understanding attained through daily practice of this sensible approach to living well provides the greatest benefit.

New Alternatives

In the Western world we went from emotional illiteracy to an obsessive concern with emotions over the period of a hundred years or so, especially as a result of Freud's influence.

The feeling focus of modern culture covers laziness, sloppy thinking, rationalization, and self-indulgence. Maybe there was a time when many people didn't recognize what they were feeling, but now there is an overemphasis on feelings as the most important element of human life. Some people seem to be attending primarily to their own feelings, building their lives around them. The need these days is not to get in touch with feelings but to get in touch with the reality of circumstances.

Consider how the word *feeling* has spilled over its natural boundaries into other areas of human existence. Some speakers say, "I feel like a hamburger for lunch." Others say, "I feel that she did commit the crime." In Japan, a major advertising campaign centered on the phrase "I feel Coke." Psychotherapists use the very convenient time-filler query "And how do you feel about that?" How lazy we have become! How undisciplined in behavior!

Constructive living doesn't ask anyone to give up feeling.

But we must beware of overindulging the feeling side of our lives. When we focus on emotions exclusively, other important aspects of living are neglected. We must balance our awareness of feelings with attentive, purposeful action in the world. "Every man feels instinctively that all the beautiful sentiments in the world weigh less than a single lovely action," wrote James Russell Lowell.

Constructive living recommends that we attend to even the smallest tasks of daily life with mindful attention. Some see a danger of constructive living as turning attention to trivial, insignificant acts, allowing an escape from important human tasks. I doubt it. There is short-term escape, to be sure, but we tire of it. There is something in us humans—call it *sei no yokubo,* as Morita did, or a desire to live fully, if you like—that calls us to more than triviality.

Until recently we seemed to have the two alternatives of (1) individual freedom with all the concomitant social ills—teenage suicides, violence, crime, unwanted pregnancies, social unrest—or (2) social control with increasing restrictions to protect and control. Now, through constructive living, we are offered a third possibility of freedom in the areas that are genuinely free and self-control in the areas that require personal and social responsibility. Constructive living doesn't make it easy to give up smoking; it doesn't produce laws that make it difficult to smoke. It merely tells you that the desire to smoke is uncontrollable and that, regardless of that desire, you smoke or you don't. Notice that there is no talk here of deciding to give up smoking or making a commitment to quit smoking or getting motivated to stop smoking. You stop or you don't. That is reality. The rest is just smoke talk.

Before, it seemed that we had the alternative of expressing feelings or suppressing them. The alternatives were couched in terms of open, honest portrayal of emotions or dishonest, unhealthy censoring of them. The third alternative presented by constructive living is honest recognition and acceptance of feelings without the requirement of behavioral expression of them.

DAVID K. REYNOLDS

Over the past twenty years, reality has demonstrated that constructive living is not only an effective method for coping with the suffering of existing neuroses, but it can be used to prevent neurosis and minimize the negative effects of stress.

BRAIN RESEARCH EVIDENCE

As Richard Restak, a neurologist, wrote in *The Washington Post,* "We are what we do rather than what we think, fantasize or otherwise inwardly experience about ourselves. . . . We are truly ourselves only when we act." He bases his assertion on recent brain research by Benjamin Libet at UCSF that indicates that subjects' brains show activity milliseconds before they become conscious of "choosing" to flex their forefingers. Moreover, the subjects can choose not to flex during the milliseconds between their awareness of their intention to move and the actual flexing. The ability to veto the brain's decision may be the locus of free will, according to Libet.

The theoretical implications for constructive living are worth considering. For decades, Moritist theory held that thoughts, feelings, and other mental events are natural phenomena, not completely under our conscious control. They are natural and spontaneous responses arising from our environments, histories, and so forth. Now we begin to see some neurophysiological evidence for the Moritist assertion. The natural environment of our minds includes our brain activity. The brain responds naturally and spontaneously to the reality that presents itself. Then the brain generates impulses that we interpret as thoughts, feelings, decisions, and the like.

Constructive-living theory holds that the locus of control in our lives lies in behavior. We define who we are by what we do. Accepting thoughts, feelings, moods, and other mental events is our only recourse; they aren't completely within our control; what else can we do but accept them? To struggle with the undefeatable is to play a losing game of life. Now there is scientific evidence supporting the theory generated from human experience. The control and freedom in our lives *do* come through what we do.

It is satisfying to find scientific support for constructive-living principles. But scientific theory changes. Experimental refutations of Libet's procedures may appear in future reports. Our experience provides solid support for our understandings that mental events aren't totally controllable by our will and that within the domain of behavior lie personal freedom and control of our lives.

The Practice of Constructive Living

Constructive-living outpatient practice integrates Morita therapy and Naikan therapy in the education of any student who is capable of learning and applying the principles. Normal people, psychotics who are properly medicated and in contact, substance abusers, depressives on proper antidepressant medication, and others can benefit from constructive living because it works to reduce unnecessary stress and suffering in everyday life. However, those who cannot learn the principles cannot be taught—i.e., people who are out of contact with reality, those with very low intelligence, very young children, and those who will not give the principles an experiential try.

THE PROPER ORDER

Both Morita and Naikan approaches are used with every student in order to provide a well-rounded educational experience. Morita therapy alone produces an action-oriented client who accomplishes purposes in spite of fears and self-doubts. But the student may have nonsocial, self-centered purposes. Naikan therapy alone produces a student who has proper gratitude and the desire to live a meaningful life by serving others in repayment for a lifetime of accumulated love and concrete favors. But the student may not have the realistic action-orientation to carry out these fine purposes. It is said that Morita therapy walks us past the rubble in our lives and Naikan therapy helps us clear away that rubble. We need both for a well-rounded existence.

The question, then, is which method should be applied first. Clinical experience indicates that people who present with difficulties in the area of social relations (trouble with spouse, neighbors, workmates, relatives) and people with substance abuse and antisocial problems benefit from Naikan elements of constructive living first. People who present with fears and phobias, anxiety, obsessions, and difficulties performing specific necessary tasks benefit from the Morita approach first. Again, in time each student will be instructed in both methods for greatest benefit.

The first session begins with an evaluation of the student's purpose in coming for help. Usually, the student comes in order to feel better about some problem in life or for some self-improvement. Unless students are allowed to talk initially in some detail about their problems, they aren't ready to listen to the instructor's guidance and the instructor doesn't know how best to tailor the teaching of the principles to the specific student's needs. But feeling-focused talking doesn't continue for long. Complaining about feelings merely turns more attention toward feelings and causes more misery for the student.

OUTPATIENT MORITA THERAPY

Outpatient Morita therapy involves teaching the student certain principles of living and inviting the student to give them a trial in the student's everyday life. Whether the principles are fully understood or not, assignments are made to allow the student increasing experiential knowledge about the constructive lifeway. For example, the student may be advised to get up at a particular time

DAVID K. REYNOLDS

whether feeling like it or not, to make the bed, prepare breakfast and eat it regardless of anxieties or dreadful anticipation of what might happen during the day. The student may be prompted to notice that while attention is focused on making the bed or preparing a meal, the symptomatic fear has been temporarily forgotten. At this initial stage of instruction, constructive activities are used to help the students distract themselves from their symptoms. Of course, the basic problem of feeling centeredness remains. In time, the student will learn to sweep the floor because the floor is dirty and not because sweeping provides a temporary escape from undesired feelings. But the immediate, temporary relief through activity is welcomed by the suffering student.

The student may be asked to report on activities and observations of external reality in great detail. This quizzing trains the student to focus attention on behavior and on the external world, in contrast to the usual habits of introspection and focus on feelings. I will ask my students to close their eyes and describe my office in detail. Beginning students have great difficulty describing the room because their attention has been on their suffering and not on observing reality. When they open their eyes, they realize that reality is much more colorful and interesting than their coded memory of it. Our goal is to help them notice and appreciate this varied reality both because it is interesting and because it keeps presenting all of us with what-needs-to-be-done.

Utilizing a similar technique, I may ask the student to report on detailed behaviors such as which foot touched the floor first when he was arising from bed, what she did on that morning with the toothpaste cap while brushing the teeth, and so forth. Beginning students haven't noticed. They try to answer in generalizations and abstractions. They were preoccupied with feelings and ruminations while carrying out everyday tasks and didn't notice what they were doing in any concrete detail. In time, they learn to do planning and reflecting and introspection at appropriate times and not all day long. The focus in our sessions is on activities and external observations and not on complaints about mental anguish. They may begin to take more notice of their surroundings and their behavior because they will be quizzed regularly on the subjects. But in time they come to see the inherent value in doing so.

A journal may be assigned. The form of the constructive-living journal is as follows: A sheet of paper is divided vertically into one narrow and two wide columns. The narrow column is headed TIME, and the wide columns are headed FEELINGS and BEHAVIOR. The students are asked to write at least a page a day, selecting any time and writing what they felt (or thought) in one column and what they did at that time in the other column. For each time selected, the students should pick a time a couple of minutes earlier (if the students pick the exact time, all that can be written in the behavior column is "writing in the journal"), while the feelings and behaviors are still fresh in memory.

Early students tend to write much in the feelings column and little in the behavior column, as though feelings are more important and worthy of description than behavior. This tendency will change during the course of instruction.

Maxims and tales are used to teach the principles in easily remembered form. For example, a constructive-living maxim is "Run to the edge of the cliff and stop on a dime." It means "Do everything you can do to bring about the goal you seek, but leave it up to fate or God or reality to determine the actual outcome of your actions." We can do all we can to achieve our purposes, but we cannot totally control the results of our actions. Still, we must keep trying. We must be clear about what is controllable and what isn't controllable in life and then direct our efforts to affect what is controllable while accepting the uncontrollable.

Reading assignments in books about constructive living and books related to the students' problems are given. Specific behavioral assignments are made and the results are discussed in each weekly session. In this constructive-living approach, we don't believe that some magical transformation takes place during the teaching hour each week. Rather, it is the hard work by the student during the week that brings about deserved and lasting change.

DAVID K. REYNOLDS

Teaching sessions may be held while walking (especially useful for depressed, inactive students), in the student's home (while cleaning it together), at the student's workplace, in a market, in a crowded building, or in an airplane, depending on the student's problem. Constructive living can also be carried out by correspondence.

The essential feature of Naikan therapy is a reflection on three themes—what was received from some person, what was done in return for that person, and what troubles and worries were caused that person—during specific periods of the student's life. The student may be asked to do Naikan reflection each morning and evening for thirty minutes, keeping a journal of what was recalled.

For example, the student may be asked to spend the first morning reflecting on the mother during the student's grammar school years. What did your mother do for you during that period? What did you do for her? What troubles and worries did you cause her during grammar school years? As always, specific and concrete details are sought. The student is to write a page about what was recalled. That evening the student is to reflect on what others did for him during the day, what he did for others, and what troubles he caused others. Again, a page is to be written. The second morning, the student continues with Naikan reflection on the mother, but this time covering the next three years of the student's life. The second evening, the student does Naikan reflection on others, covering the second day's events. And so on. When the student finishes reflection on the mother until she died or up to the present, he begins again with the father during the student's grammar school years. Eventually, the student will be asked to do Naikan reflection on the persons with whom he has interpersonal difficulties (spouse, fellow workers, and so forth).

The daily journal entries are brought to the weekly session, where the students read them aloud to the instructor. The instructor makes no comment or evaluation or interpretation. The instructor only listens and thanks the students for their efforts, encouraging the students to continue the Naikan for another week until all the necessary persons have been considered in a Naikan light.

Additional assignments include cleaning drawers, ten thank-yous, secret services, picking up public trash, gift giving, and thank-you letters. Cleaning drawers means taking everything from a drawer or chest, cleaning the empty drawer, then returning each item to the drawer after cleaning it and thanking it for some specific service it performed for the student. For example, "Thank you, ladle, for helping me serve the soup to my family last night." Clothing, office equipment, and books also serve us in ways that deserve our cleaning and appreciation.

Quarreling couples are assigned the task of saying thank you to each other ten times a day. They must keep a record of the ten times. They need not feel gratitude (uncontrollable directly by will), but they must say the words appropriately (controllable behavior). Similarly, quarreling persons may be assigned the doing of secret services for each other, the bringing of gifts to one another, or the writing of thank-you letters (for specific past acts) to distant relatives. Cleaning up public litter is a chance to repay one's neighbors and fellow citizens for the services they perform daily for us.

Naikan reflection can be extended to people whose faces we have never seen and whose names we don't know (such as the people who made the chairs we sit in and those who make the ink for our typewriters, computers, and pens), to objects (the pens that serve us well), and to energy (electricity, for example). We can learn to consider what we have done in return for water and electricity and paper and our shoes as well as what we have done in return for those people close to us.

INPATIENT MORITA AND NAIKAN THERAPIES

Inpatient Morita and Naikan therapies are not ordinarily practiced as part of constructive living in the West. They are still practiced in Japan, however.

DAVID K. REYNOLDS

Inpatient Morita Therapy

Inpatient Morita therapy begins with a week of isolated bed rest. Within the Moritist hospital the patient is not permitted to read or write or converse or smoke or engage in any distraction other than eating three meals a day and taking care of other natural body functions. There is no escape from the waves of doubt, boredom, anxiety, regret, and the like that pass through the mind (more accurately, they are the mind in that setting.) Past failures are reviewed mentally, along with future potential troubles. Despite the suffering, time passes and the patient survives. Feelings and thoughts well up and fade. The patient learns some measure of acceptance of these mental phenomena. And the patient becomes bored. It is unnatural to lie in retreat from the world when one is physically capable of constructive activity. The desire to move about emerges.

Subsequent stages of inpatient Morita therapy offer the patient scaled tasks, including weeding the garden, writing a journal of activities, participating in group sports, household chores, errands off the hospital grounds and, finally, return to everyday life outside the hospital. The patient is encouraged to pay attention to the surroundings so as to discover what needs doing and then do it. Constructive activity provides a distraction from rumination about neurotic misery. In time, reality's tasks are carried out simply because they need to be done, whether the symptoms are present or not. In fact, the subjective experience of symptoms declines over time; but that decline is merely a pleasant byproduct of being able to do what needs doing while suffering or not.

The entire period of hospitalization varies considerably from place to place and patient to patient. Perhaps two or three months is the mean these days, although Morita himself began inpatient treatment in the 1920s with a period of about one month.

Inpatient Naikan Therapy

Inpatient Naikan involves a week of intensive reflection on three themes: what was received from some person; what was done in return for that person; and what troubles and worries were caused that person. The Naikan client spends each day from early morning until night in isolated reflection on these themes. At first, the mother or mother surrogate is the object of reflection. What did my mother do for me during the first three years of grammar school? What did I do in return for her? What troubles did I cause her? After a period of time, perhaps an hour or two, the therapist comes to listen to the Naikan client's accounting of what was recalled. The therapist listens gratefully, without comment or interpretation. Then, during the next period of Naikan meditation, the same three themes will be considered regarding the mother during the client's fourth through sixth grade years. Again, the therapist comes to listen. The pattern progresses in approximately three-year intervals up to the present or until the mother died. Then the client begins again with the grammar school period, working on the recollections of the father in the same sequence. Working from the past up to the present, the client works on other significant persons in his or her life.

The method is simple, but it has a very powerful emotional impact on the clients. In effect, they measure themselves by their own standards of reciprocity and find themselves failing. There is no escape into the deflection that they are being tested by someone else's standards (some formal religious code, for example, such as the Ten Commandments). Guilt and gratitude and a sense of having been loved in spite of one's failings and the desire to try to repay others are common results of inpatient Naikan.

After the week is over, clients are encouraged to continue Naikan during shorter periods each day. Each morning, the client is to continue reflections about others in the past just as during the hospital period. In the evening, the client is advised to reflect about that day—what was received from others during the day, what was returned to them, and what troubles the client caused others during the day.

The Essence of Constructive Living

What are the absolutely essential elements of constructive living? What defines it as a unique lifeway or therapeutic method? How does one know whether a technique fits within the framework of constructive living?

Let me say a few words about what is not essential to constructive living. As far as I can see, there are some characteristic techniques but no specific techniques that are essential. We can do constructive living without doing absolute bed rest as in Morita therapy and without seated meditation as in Naikan. We can do constructive living without diary guidance or reading assignments.

There is nothing particularly Japanese about constructive living. It isn't necessary to use foreign words like *shinkeishitsu* or *toraware* or even Morita or Yoshimoto. There is no requirement that our students be interested in Zen or things Japanese.

So what is left? As far as I can see, there are a few essential principles, orientations, and a small class of techniques that constitute the core of constructive living.

Reality Focus

Reality must be accepted as it is. Feelings are a natural part of reality. It follows that they must be accepted, without direct struggle.

Both Morita and Naikan ask us to look at reality. They are realistic. And both lead us to act on reality. It isn't enough to ponder, to ruminate, to intellectualize, to imagine. We must take what we know into the world and apply it in order to keep learning, growing, living.

Some suffering in the world is based on real problems. Some suffering is based on excessive self-focus and experiential ignorance. The solution to the latter suffering is experience-based education.

The essential goal of constructive living is to see reality clearly. We haven't paid proper attention (Morita), have inadvertently misperceived it (Morita), or have selfishly misperceived it (Naikan).

A side effect of the Morita lifeway may be reduction in symptoms or suffering. It may be a new appreciation of the colors and variety in nature. A side effect of Naikan may be gratitude or guilt or some other feeling. It may be a resolve to repay the world or clean up one's life or sweep the sidewalk. But both require us to recognize and encounter specific, concrete, detailed reality. They discourage overuse of abstraction, generalization, and vagueness.

Action/Experiential Orientation

Constructive living emphasizes the need to put what is learned into life activity every day. Morita and Naikan aren't lifeways that ultimately remove us from the world into some nonproductive, withdrawn existence. They are at their best and most useful as we operate in everyday life.

Behavior is the controllable aspect of reality. It is through purposeful, realistic behavior that we work to change reality. We are responsible for what we do no matter what we feel. A few phenomena (some people include them in the category of behaviors) such as stuttering, trembling, and impotence are not directly controllable by the will. They are considered to be uncontrollable expressions (like feelings) and must be accepted as they are while the student works on controllable behaviors.

Attention must be focused on reality. Reality is the proper teacher of life's lessons. Observation of reality results in information about what needs to be done (i.e., purposeful behavior). When what needs to be done isn't clear, Morita can suggest only to do what is clear. That is part of the reason for the structured nature of Zen monasteries. One's situation, when properly structured, presents what needs doing in relatively routine and clear fashion so that attention can be invested in doing activities well. The simple and organized life reduces the attention necessary for deciding what needs doing.

The constructive-living approach to the issue of knowing what needs doing includes the organization and simplification of Morita and Zen but also the moral investigation of Naikan. Naikan introspection helps us to discover, even in the most complex situation, what needs to be done. Naikan provides a moral compass for determining what needs to be done. Then the Morita practice helps us become people who actually do it.

Intellectual understanding may be helpful on some level, but action-grounded experiential understanding is of greater dependability and benefit. Action on reality teaches truth. Reflection on the past and planning for the future may provide useful insights and valuable preparations, but excessive rumination and daydreaming are self-centered and harmful.

No-Self

Constructive living shows us no-self. Morita shows how we merge with our environments. We are reality's way of getting reality's work done. As we fit ourselves to the situations we encounter we become the situations, harmonized in a way that reduces conflict and misery. Naikan reveals how much of our self is borrowed from others.

Foundation of Religion

Both say that they aren't religion but that they will direct us to the foundation of the religious impulse. We become better Christians or Jews or Muslims or Buddhists for having studied these lifeways.

The Lifeway, Not the Teacher

Both Morita and Naikan emphasize the method and not the teacher. They direct us to develop our own potential without dependence on some other person with supposedly superior powers. The instructor is merely a guide, a sounding board, an adviser. Zen teachers, too, talk about the finger pointing at the moon. "I'm only the pointing finger," they say, "not the moon. Don't confuse the two."

Characteristic orientations mark the teacher/practitioner of constructive living. Most notable is the lack of separation between the teacher's life and the lifeway he or she teaches. Constructive living is not an approach to helping others that is used only in the office setting. It permeates the life.

Educational Model

The model underlying the practice of constructive living is educational, not medical. We prefer to use terms such as *student, teacher, guidance, habit, graduation,* and the like to terms such as *patient, therapist, healing, symptom,* and *cure.*

Acceptance is a key attitude modeled by the teacher/guide. Genuine acceptance naturally leads to gratitude and a desire to serve others. Constructive action is a natural part of the whole. The guide is reality-centered, reality-confident.

During the teaching sessions the guide is constantly engaged in turning the student's attention toward reality.

REPRESENTATIVE TECHNIQUES

Characteristic techniques are employed in constructive living, but perhaps no single technique is essential. Any method that pro-

DAVID K. REYNOLDS

motes the student's constructive learning from reality may be used.

Experiential assignments such as cleaning a public park or telephoning for a job interview or writing a letter of thanks or shopping for fresh vegetables may be made. Daily journal assignments are common, with multiple columns and behaviors recorded separately from feelings.

A detailed review of recent behaviors and their results and quizzes about the details of surroundings help redirect the student's attention away from feeling-centered self-focus.

Constructive-living instructors often use the principle of yielding, more or less as it is used in the martial arts. Rather than meeting the force of the student's misconceptions head-on, the instructor uses the student's own energy, deflecting it in a desired direction. For example, "You say that you are a perfectionist, but you aren't nearly perfectionistic enough. You haven't noticed the fire exits in this room. Be more perfectionistic in your observation of your surroundings." "You complain of guilt, but what you do to cause the guilt hasn't changed. You need more guilt." With these unexpected remarks and the subsequent changes in behavior, the student comes to view mental states as acceptable as they are.

The teacher/guide may listen, advise, offer koans for reflection, assign readings, take walks with the student, go shopping with the student, help clean the student's room or office, attend the student's wedding ceremony. Always, the teacher reflects reality back to the student and encourages the student to recognize it and act on it positively.

CONCLUSION

Other teachers of constructive living might emphasize different aspects of the practice, but we would agree on these core concepts and methods. It is reassuring that in order to teach this lifeway to others we need not be perfect, provided we are realistic.

Facts of Life

A recent advertisement in a popular magazine asks if the reader eats too much, then diets, fasts, or vomits. The ad continues: "You may have thought it was your fault. But it isn't. Chances are you have an eating disorder. And if you do, no amount of willpower will help you control it."

The ad is wrong. The only thing that will control overeating is to eat less. In our strange folk way of talking, we say that we eat less because of willpower. To label something an eating disorder makes it no more medical than to label jealousy an emotional disorder or to label filth a bathing disorder or to label smoking or drinking alcohol an addictive disorder or to label poor manners an etiquette disorder. They are all the same in that they share problems of behavior, of doing. They are brought under control by doing something differently. You know that.

But we hope to suffer from something easily corrected, something curable through medical or psychological magic: a pill, perhaps, or a few sessions with a professional whose expertise will make our problem disappear like a bad dream would be just right. It is time to grow up and face the real situation. When we have behaved ourselves into destructive habits we must behave ourselves out of them. There is no psychological sorcery that will make it easy for us to change what we do. But change we must if we are to be the best we can be.

Costly and time-consuming analysis of the sources of our "disorders" is rather interesting. It provides reasons (read "excuses") for our problems; most of these reasons lie outside of our control. How reassuring to know the origins of our limits are someone else's errors! Still, it remains for us to change what we do.

Well then, how do we begin to change our poor habits of behavior? How do we develop this wonderful willpower? Frankly, I have no idea. The process is so complicated. I suspect no one else knows, either, though some claim to have mastered the understanding of this elusive matter. What I do know is what needs doing. What needs doing is to have a goal, to accept whatever uncontrollable factors come along to help or hinder in achieving that goal, and to work toward that goal. In other words: Know your purpose; accept reality (including your feelings); and do what needs doing. If you have been studying the constructive lifeway, you have heard this advice over and over again.

THE WAY IT IS

No matter what personal-growth method or psychotherapy you may try, many of life's tasks will never become fun. Taking in the car for servicing, sending off an application for a school transcript, studying an uninteresting subject, waiting for the plumber to arrive, cleaning up a spilled bowl of soup—these activities aren't pleasurable whether or not one is enlightened. To expect some discipline or philosophy to make them enjoyable is rather childish. But do them we must. Enjoyable or not.

Conversely, to try to assert that sexual gratification or eating one's favorite foods or experiencing the rush of an illicit drug isn't pleasurable is equal foolishness. We cannot dictate our feelings one way or the other. We must accept them as they are and still get the car serviced, refrain from overeating, study the uninteresting material, and avoid the chemicals that harm us. No elaborate definitions or theories will make hard struggle easy.

REALITY AND TALK ABOUT REALITY

My impression is that most people want change in their lives because they haven't mastered who they are now or where they are now, because they're not doing well with what they have. How about mastering what is now and then changing?

I sometimes see "healers" trying to force their clients' words and lives into schema. The schema are more or less complicated, but they are limited conceptual models of what reality ought to be. Reality isn't any of their models. To the extent that a healer realizes this truth, the healer is wise.

More than ideas, I love reality.

Better to master these simple levels of encountered reality before trying to understand or master more complex ideational schemes. I suspect that high-level philosophical wordplay gets society's attention and rewards because it helps distract people from ineptness at doing well in concrete reality. It is easier to ponder the meaning of life than to fold towels neatly over and over again.

Whether we are drunk or sober, failing or succeeding, reality keeps steadily on. Whatever philosophers or gurus or seers say, reality keeps steadily on. Solid, reliable reality. The word *reliable* here has a particular meaning. Don't misinterpret it.

FUNDAMENTALS

Some people try to make constructive living a strategy for temporarily accepting the naturalness of feelings while working to "improve" themselves so that feelings of anger, frustration, lack of confidence, despair, and the like don't occur (or are reduced) in their lives. They both lie to themselves and miss the point. Feelings are *natural*. This moment's feelings fit this moment's me-reality; they are a natural element in this now.

DAVID K. REYNOLDS

Some constructive-living students define their life crises as exceptional cases. They want to call time-out and return to old ways of handling their dilemma. They lose the sound basis for action provided by constructive living. They don't see that a life crisis fits their practice just like keeping a constructive-living journal or working on a koan or dusting or driving. There is something to be done about the reality that includes the crisis that faces them. Accept feelings; know purpose; take action.

Too often we seem to substitute theory for action. And our theories become further and further separated from everyday reality. In psychology, for example, we have elaborate theories about subtle functions of the mind, but we don't teach fundamental principles such as the principles that feelings fade over time, feelings keep changing, behavior is directly controllable and feelings are not.

In religion we have both intricate theological theories and personal-experiential approaches to God but little apparent awareness of reality's contributions to our everyday existence. There is little emphasis on the concrete support we get from other people every day, little attention to the fact that our very existence depended and depends on others' efforts in our behalf. In sociology we have complex theories of social interaction, but our society suffers from social problems that could be solved with the knowledge we have already. In economics we have abundant theories on macro and micro levels, but we have a huge national debt and an unbelievable amount of personal debt.

Why is it that we have skipped fundamental truths about action and reality in order to develop complicated theories based on constructions of the mind?

The Working Mind

Minds process information. That's what minds do. When there is no information to process, the mind invents information through a function we call imagination.

A middle-aged lady found herself back in social circulation. She put on makeup, fixed her hair, dressed appropriately, then worried about what might happen at the party that night. What if? Would he? Might they? Her mind was generating scenarios to work on. In a few hours, reality would give her mind real data to work on. In the meantime, her mind needed something to do. She didn't know about keeping it busy with real information while waiting for her escort to pick her up.

Put yourself in a quiet room long enough and your mind will generate sounds. Put yourself in a dark room and, in time, you will see things. Put a stationary light in that dark room and your mind will imagine the light is moving. The mind seeks information and will generate it when enough isn't forthcoming from reality.

When we don't want to be carried away with imagining, we can assure a flow of reality-based information through proper behavior and attention to attention. Moving our bodies increases the likelihood of inputting information from reality—a stroll through our neighborhood or a park, a vacation, volunteer work, attending evening classes. Isolating ourselves provides fruitful opportunities for imagination to work. When I write, for example, it is best for me to be alone. But in general, when we want less imagining, it is helpful to be interacting with other people. Being around others won't eliminate the function of imagination, but it will give it some realistic information to work on. Imagination is related to procrastination, but that topic is too broad to consider here. It will be dealt with later in this section.

We can notice our habits of daydreaming and our tendencies to worry about illusory incidents. We have some control over bringing our attention back to our immediate surroundings. Physical activity seems to help. It is easier to outline and underline a book than to simply read it. It is easier still to refinish an antique chair than to read. And so forth. There is something about physical activity that facilitates pulling our attention to reality and away from imagination.

As I walk through the forest, my mind seeks the variety that nature provides. Then it looks for the orderliness of pattern. My mind needs both variety and order. I suspect that yours does, too. Reality provides both variety and order; so does imagination.

GENERATING PREOCCUPATIONS

Toraware is nonacceptance, a kind of artificial attachment to one aspect of reality and a concomitant rejection of other elements of natural reality. Hasegawa Yozo, a leader in the Morita mental health movement in Japan, made a theoretical contribution to the understanding of *toraware* that moved it out of the narrow psychiatric concern for obsession with neurotic symptoms into the broader realm of obsession with work or love or even preoccupation with Morita's ideas. I doubt that Hasegawa realized at the time the monumental theoretical step he was taking, but the credit is his.

Toraware narrows the spotlight of the mind to some aspect of life and shuts out other aspects. It is contrasted with the open acceptance of reality and the flowing mind that moves naturally to attend to a variety of stimuli. The broadest domain for the opposite of *toraware* is the acceptance and nonattachment in Zen-Taoism.

Attachment or *toraware* means applying some artificial mental construct to what is, and then being more attracted to the construct than to reality. It is a sort of mental clouding of vision of reality.

We live in a complex world. There are many possible goals for us, many ways to act to achieve those goals. We are pulled by all sorts of voices from about and within us. To more or less single-mindedly focus in on a single goal or class of goals gives direction to our living, even when that direction is destructive. Few people seem to notice that one of the allures of drugs is the single-minded devotion to securing them. If the addict can just get the next fix, that is sufficient in life. Contrast that goal with the middle-aged businessman aiming to pay off debts, buy a new car, please his wife, understand his children, keep from getting too flabby, and so forth.

Considering the frequency with which paranoia is encountered in normal and mentally disordered people, there is relatively little written about this form of suffering. The delusion that someone else is plotting to do one harm can be found to some degree in everyone at one time or another. The boundary between paranoia and a realistic appraisal of our enemies' interests may be unclear at times. The thesis here is simply that obsessions with drugs (including alcohol), sex, money, love, paranoia, and the like are foci for simplifying the organization of stimulus input from the world and providing a limited set of goals from the spectrum of goals reality offers us. In other words drugs, sex, money, love, and paranoia serve to help some people focus their attention on a limited set of information from their sensory input, to make clear (though sometimes incorrect) sense of that information, and to limit the range of relevant goals.

Just as the lover "reads into" the loved one's acts gestures of concern and affection, so the paranoid individual sees threat in others' behavior. All the world loves a lover, we say. The lover throws the net of simplification wide, seeing affection and tolerance in everyone. Similarly, the paranoid person expands the strategy for understanding a particular foe to encompass everyone around. We need not posit a psychological mechanism of projection here. The lover does not attribute his love to others. His love is quite different from that which he supposes others to possess.

Obsession with money, fame, food, or whatever acts to simplify the decision-making process in a complicated world. Obsession "boils down" reality to a rigid, bit-size chunk . . . that is no longer reality.

Morita noticed that when *shinkeishitsu* neurotics in Japan said, "I shouldn't feel nervous," they implied, I need more willpower to control my feelings; I lack character and moral fiber for feeling this way. Our American neurotics also say, "I shouldn't feel nervous." But behind the Westerners' words are the thoughts I don't have my life together; I need a better background or a better therapy. The Japanese people in neurotic moments tend to see the flaws in themselves. The American people in neurotic moments tend to see the flaws in their upbringing, their circumstances, their lack of appropriate social or psychotherapeutic support. Both, however, see the anxiety or fear or obsession as the undesirable outcome of the flaw. Neither sees the anxiety or fear or obsession as natural, with both positive and negative aspects. And from a larger perspective, both are preoccupied (obsessed, caught) in the *toraware* of trying to cure (overcome, fix) their neurotic suffering.

Life Wisdom Notes

There follow some random notes on a variety of subjects from a constructive living point of view.

THE LONG VIEW

Let's consider the usefulness of taking on tasks that can't be completed in a lifetime. What are the implications for our perspective on our daily lives? Current views seem to emphasize immediacy. The emphasis in our world is on instant satisfaction, instant success. Consider how some of our current culture heroes are lottery winners, game-show contestants, youthful entrepreneurs, and entertainment stars. They achieve their success quickly, with what appears to be effortless ease.

When I am on the island of Kauai, I can help with watering and weeding the garden, but I must depend on others to carry on the task that goes beyond my stay on the island and beyond any one person's life, for that matter. The garden can provide sustenance for many generations. Its existence marks tasks and harvests beyond my limited capabilities. My work in the garden is part of that extended pursuit. So is my writing this book.

Being part of these longer boulevards of activity alters our perspective on ourselves as participants in this world. The setback that strikes me right now is both the most important thing in the world and a relatively minor detour in the boulevard along which I walk. We'll put off the subject of procrastination until later in this section.

I am reminded of my dependence on others for achieving goals that lie beyond my reach. How can I be so attached to my minute personal obsessions when these larger goals are of so much more consequence than this moment's petty myopic objectives?

EXCESS OF SELF

We live in an age of an excess of self, an unfortunate obsession because it's an empty one.

Still, there is nothing wrong with you as you are now. You are mistaken in believing you need future enlightenment or future cure or even future self-improvement. You don't yet recognize who or what or where you are. The you that you imagine needs upgrading is not your self.

One meaning of the phrase "You are already a Buddha" is that the mind in its basic natural form is already fine just as it is. It may need education if it has drifted from its original common-sense understanding and purposes. Behavior, on the other hand, may need correction; it may not be all right in its current form. Then how can I say "You are what you do"?

Think about it.

Why must people seek special experiences? Why do they long to be what they will never be, cannot be? Why do they try to fill their minds and lives with foolish esoterica?

We suggest that all we need to do with our lives is "simply" to do what needs doing. Why? Because it needs doing. We can philosophize about the identity of doer-doing-object, to put it in Western terms. Or we can talk about just doing, to put it in Zen terms. Such talk is no more than a pleasant diversion. The important thing is doing.

Some students of constructive living try to make a show to others of what is happening in their minds. They make efforts to demonstrate that they are doing something mindfully, with full attention. When they try to communicate that they are acting mindfully, they are adding something to the smooth functioning of their purposeful behavior. They look awkward. The doing itself is sufficient.

INSIGHT

Recognizing and understanding our tendencies doesn't excuse them. Some people seem to believe that insight into their self-centered habits is a substitute for correcting them. Some readers will believe that they have mastered something important when they read the above sentence. Insight and understanding, like potential, are cheap. Whatever you have heard about the "being" of human beings, it is our doing that gives us meaning and identity in the world. In our action on reality we discover reality's response and we discover who we are. The issue of whether Mr. Smith is truly angry at his wife or displacing anger at his boss onto his wife only comes up as long as Mr. Smith abuses his wife. When he stops doing angry things to his wife, the issue of displacement disappears.

The words *path* or *way* (*tao* in Chinese, *dô* in Japanese) imply travel, movement, action. No one calls Zen or Taoism or Aikido or Judo "the bench" or "the chair." These lifeways and arts are called the path or the way. The element of action is essential to all of them, not merely seated contemplation or reflection or clear insight.

WHIRLING DUST

How much of modern life is the equivalent of studying outdated television listings, listening to recordings of last week's traffic and weather reports, clipping expired coupons from yellowed newspapers?

How much of modern life is just allowing information to flow through, filling mental time? We're not yet ready to deal fully with the issue of procrastination here. What is the clear purpose in reading a newspaper or watching a commercial on television?

When did modern life begin to be replete with word laxatives, swallowed and, well, passed? Smoothly, effortlessly.

Did it begin with advertising? With marketing decisions that passed along slick, soft slop? Not altogether; why look only at others? When did we begin to slurp our mental soup?

Many people prefer to gather more information than to act on the information they already possess. Now, I have no objection to gathering information, of course. However, the gathering of data from the library of everyday can continue to the degree that life's term papers don't get written. We can flood ourselves into immobility with masses of information. We must know our purposes. If our data gathering is aimed at putting off necessary action, we must shift gears.

GOD TALK

Some of my readers have noted a trend in my writing toward the mystical, toward the spiritual. If that is so, it is regrettable. Because it means that I am using words that make some part of everyday experience look like it is set apart—mystical, spiritual, religious. But there is only everyday experience. If there is to be religion, it must be woven through that everyday experience and not set aside in some special Sunday-morning category. It must avoid association with the philosophy section in bookstores and particular types of church or temple architecture; it must shun special garb such as robes and a special vocabulary that only the elite inner circle has learned. We must discover that religion, like ourselves, is nothing special.

If there is a spiritual thread woven through constructive living, then where are the clues that signal its existence? If you mean how many times the word G-o-d comes up in my writings, then the answer is very, very rarely. But if you mean how many times God appears in my writings, then the answer is quite often. My guess is that you have never laid eyes on this being you call God in the sense of having actually seen some form (bearded old man, earth mother, or whatever). All you have seen is that stream of awareness that is you. That stream of awareness comes from reality.

Constructive-living writing is about that reality. Constructive-living writing is part of that reality. If you are searching for God, you must find that being within your stream of awareness. There is nothing else, no other place to find God.

PURPOSE AND MOTIVATION

Elsewhere I have discussed the inadequacies of motivational explanations of human behavior. We can offer layers of reasons why we do as we do. That man is suicidal because he has job problems, because he lacks confidence in himself, because he was abused as a child, because he is fixated at a particular psychosexual stage of development, because he has a narcissistic personality. Along with C. Wright Mills (1940), I see such talk about the reasons for behavior to be socially learned and without explanatory or predictive power. In other words, we learn socially acceptable reasons to offer others in explanation for what we do so that people stop asking us why we did what we did.

"Bobby, why did you hit your little sister?"

"Because I was hungry."

"Now, Bobby, why did you really hit your little sister?"

"Because I hate her," or "Because I love to tease," or "Because I'm naughty."

However unsatisfactory our explanations of why people do what they do, we seem to need to be able to talk in some way about the direction of our behavior. In constructive living, we use the concept of purpose to talk about such directed behavior. Rather than some push of a hidden motivation, we talk about the pull of some goal.

HUMANIZING BUSINESS TRANSACTIONS

March 14

Dear Mr. and Mrs. R,

We sent the signed papers and escrow check to the title company today.

This is just a note to let you know how much we appreci-

DAVID K. REYNOLDS

ate the immaculate care with which you kept your home. That care weighed importantly in our decision to make you an offer. We have lived in apartments and condominiums until now. Your home will be our first real home. We promise to show it the same consideration you have.

We hope you enjoy your stay there until you find your next home.

If you have any tips about the upkeep would you pass them along to us or through the realtor? Thank you.

This letter is an example of a business transaction that has taken a turn for the personal. It is a step toward refusing to allow a part of life (in this case, business) to be set apart from the rest of life. I have the same objection to setting apart the business world that I have to setting apart religion from everyday life.

It appears simpler to categorize aspects of our existence temporally and behaviorally. We can then choose times and places to aim only at profits or only at worship. Such apportionment, however, is artificial and, moreover, dangerous. Reality presents us with no such artificial boundaries. We end up with the dilemma of integrating unnaturally bounded elements of our lives. We ruin the environment while getting rich. We lose our families while progressing up the corporate ladder. We sell weapons in order to buy cars and pay taxes and give aid to the victims of wars. It is very strange, this partitioning approach to life.

As an anthropologist, I was taught that cultural life was all of a piece—that religion and economics and politics and values and child rearing and other aspects of culture fit together as a mutually reinforcing whole. There were debates in anthropology about whether this felicitous whole was in the minds of the culture members or in the minds of the anthropologists who studied them. However, those who looked for an undivided totality could find it. I believe it is important that we not lose sight of that holistic view of life; moreover, that we not lose living life from that perspective.

Business is business, we hear. Don't believe it. Business is more than business. It is part of the whole of our lives.

In an interview held in May 1986, the highly regarded Moritist and former professor of Jikei University Takehisa Kora offered the following observations:

For neurotics, preparation for a task becomes a purpose in itself. They keep inserting extra steps before undertaking a pursuit. For example, in Kora's student days he would go to take a relaxing bath in order to prepare his mind for studying. Then he would feel too relaxed from the bath to study. Again, the hindrance of procrastination is evident; we'll consider it below.

The neurotic patients who come to study with Dr. Kora want specific rules for all situations so that they can act appropriately. They ask Dr. Kora if they should wear a hat when it is cold. When it is hot? Should they wear a hat when sweeping dust? How about when a person in the next room is sweeping dust? They want specific, concrete, authoritative, rule-based advice about the most trivial circumstances. They need to learn to watch reality and see what reality tells them to do.

When you see two girls looking your way, talking and laughing, you may think they are criticizing you or that they think you are cute. Both interpretations fail the test of being reality-based. The reality is that you can't hear what they are saying.

SCATTERED LESSONS FROM REALITY

When you're in a hurry, slow down and act carefully.

Never paint a sink.

Couriers and repairmen rarely come on time.

Never let a boiling pot out of your sight.

Lovemaking decreases as aging increases.

Look for the cause of a problem in yourself before looking to blame others.

If an electrical appliance isn't working, check to see that it's plugged in properly.

Don't trust people who don't attend to details.

DAVID K. REYNOLDS

Everyone becomes *shinkeishitsu* neurotic when physically ill.

Reasons for attending to reality: It is interesting; it is true; it tells you what needs doing; it is you.

Great doubt leads to great enlightenment doesn't mean what many people take it to mean.

Do the above lessons seem unrelated to one another? Think again.

REIFICATIONS

I cannot show you time any more than I can show you mind or personality or society or culture. They are all concepts, more or less useful for certain conversations or other tasks. What I argue is that some of these concepts have been improperly reified and used as explanations for all sorts of human behavior.

How often I hear, "Your presentation was very interesting. I've been doing this all along. Now I have a name for it." How often the speaker is wrong.

SECRETS

It may disappoint you, but those wonderful, hidden secrets you've stored away to be revealed only to some special someone, if at all, are of no more worth than the other experiences of your past. The secrets haven't molded you; your behaviors have.

TALK

A *shinkeishitsu* neurotic fellow comes to a fork in the road. One sign points toward "cure." The other sign points toward "discussion about cure." The *shinkeishitsu* fellow takes the latter road.

TIME OUT

We need time out for ourselves, but not for our sake. Our rest and recreation are for others' sake. We need a long-term perspective on helping. A person who gives away every cent to the poor may become a burden on others when he or she becomes old. People whose charitable contributions result in no savings or assets can drain relatives and friends.

FEELINGS

Occasionally I meet people (most often women, but sometimes men) who seem to believe that being touched or moved by something validates its importance. They speak of being moved in voices that echo holiness. It is fine to feel deeply or not. It is natural. But feelings, any feelings, provide only information, not validation. They pass. Always. When a big wave comes at me, whether feeling exalted by it or not, I must act.

COMPUTERS

For computer buffs, an analogy: Constructive living is not a ram-resident pop-up program (although some people try to use it as such). It is an operating system.

AGREEMENT

A great deal of the time you will probably agree with what you read in my writings. Now and again you may come across some notion that prompts strong disagreement. It may be that I am wrong about that notion; or it may be that you are wrong about it. In either case, don't dismiss all the other content when you find even one notion that brings forth objection.

PROCRASTINATION

We might later get to that topic, procrastination.

Did it irritate you to find the discussion of this subject put off again and again in this section? How do your moments of procrastination affect others who wait for your action?

DAVID K. REYNOLDS

The Art of Psychotherapy

WHAT IS PSYCHOTHERAPY?

Let us consider the business of training psychotherapists. First, it seems important to reflect upon the training of those who now train others. Looking back fifty years or so, there were no training facilities or systematized training courses for psychotherapists. The principles now being taught fledgling therapists have been worked out from the experiences (and observations of successes and mistakes) of therapists through trial and error. In time, their collected reminiscences became dogma. There is much to be said for the occasional rediscovery and validation of these principles from scratch by selected individuals.

But remember that all the while the practice of psychotherapy was evolving, at each point in time, the therapists acted as though they knew what they were doing, that they were on top of the field, in control of the subject matter. Yet the practice changed drastically over time. Such consideration prompts wonder whether current psychotherapists really know what they are about.

Be that as it may, becoming a psychotherapist becomes more and more difficult. Licensing requires more and more supervised hours. Exams are formidable, requiring special cram courses for preparation. One can see these increasingly severe qualifiers as important means of assuring quality control in psychotherapy or as the means by which those in power limit their competition. There is no doubt that a therapy establishment exists. As with most institutionalized establishments, it is important to keep asking for whose benefit it exists. Psychotherapy is such an amorphous pursuit that there are no guarantees of quality because there is no agreement on goals or standards and no agreement on ways to test success, whatever that might be.

MENTAL HEALTH IMPAIRMENTS

A large percentage of those who practice respectable psychotherapy in the West are psychologists with doctorates from universities. Their doctorates required long training in research methods and some original dissertation research. Asking psychologists trained in research to conduct psychotherapy is rather like asking a chemist to cook a meal: The expertise in chemistry can actually interfere with the cooking. Not necessarily, of course.

When I begin workshops in constructive living, I usually warn mental-health professionals that I consider them handicapped in their understanding of constructive living principles. Their training may deceive them into believing that they have already mastered the most important aspects of human psychology. They may try to fit constructive-living principles into some schema they have learned already elsewhere. It is almost always a mistake of distortion to attempt to do so. Fortunately, mental-health training doesn't take away life experiences. So part of the mind of the most intensively trained mental health professional still retains the possibility of evaluating the importance of constructive-living principles in some naive experiential sense. Western psychotherapies' obsession with feelings results in a roundabout course of life. There is a more straightforward approach to accomplishing a meaningful and satisfying life, which can be discovered through giving it a try.

Another reason for bringing up the handicap of mental-health

DAVID K. REYNOLDS

training during the beginning sessions of workshops is to emphasize the common human ground of the participants. Some participants may be overly impressed by the professionals' credentials
were it not for such leveling talk.

Some editors and sponsors recommend that I refrain from alie-
nating certain mental-health professionals. But I don't mind alie-
nating those whose minds are closed, those whose investment in
doing less than the best prevents them from looking at reality.
Those psychotherapists who are humble and open to reality will
see the value of this lifeway. Thomas Szasz and R. D. Laing are
examples of others who have written straightforwardly and nontra-
ditionally about their observations of psychotherapy.

At times I imagine the difficulty clinical psychologists or psychiatrists or academics might have evaluating constructive living.
Because its principles are so different from what is taught in Western psychology courses, it would be convenient to dismiss constructive living as a sort of flaky Southern California Oriental pop
fad. It is difficult to dismiss constructive living out of hand, however, because a number of books about it have been published by
respected university presses—the University of California Press,
the University of Chicago Press, the University of Hawaii Press,
and SUNY Press are examples. Articles and chapters about constructive living appear in respected scientific journals and edited
collections. Media coverage in *Vogue, The New York Times, The
Los Angeles Times, East West Magazine,* the *Los Angeles Weekly,*
the *Honolulu Star Bulletin,* and local newspapers is easier to disre-
gard for the scholar. Nevertheless such exposure keeps constructive living before the public's eye, so the topic becomes harder to
ignore year by year.

And my credentials aren't typical of someone who might be
dismissed as an upstart guru. My Ph.D. is from UCLA, and I have
taught on the faculty at the UCLA School of Public Health, the
USC School of Medicine, and the University of Houston and have
conducted grand rounds at medical facilities at UCLA, USC, Bay-
lor, and in Japan. Two research Fulbrights to Japan, research ap-

pointments at Japan's NIMH and the Tokyo Metropolitan Institute of Gerontology, and sponsorship by the World Health Organization to teach constructive living to psychiatrists in the People's Republic of China add some weight to the credentials.

But more than the paperweight of credentials, constructive-living books and articles continually ask the reader to check out constructive-living principles with the experience of everyday life. Because constructive-living principles are derived from the open-eyed observation of everyday life, it is unlikely that a reader will find anything but confirmation when that comparison occurs. That correspondence between constructive-living theory and the experience of everyday life is the fundamental strength of the method. There is no need for suspension of doubt in order to encompass some mystical or medical approach to living. Constructive living promotes a down-to-earth, practical, easily recognized view of life.

RESEARCH EVIDENCE

I am not alone in denying the value of verbal exchange as the solution to human suffering. In the final appendix to *The Myth of Neurosis*, Garth Wood straightforwardly demolishes the practice of insight psychotherapy. Wood cites a long series of quite respectable scholarly studies showing that psychotherapy reduces suffering no more than waiting for time to pass or engaging in other activities or working with amateurs rather than costly professionals. In fact there is some evidence that insight therapies actually *hinder* the relief of some distress. And at least one study showed 3 to 6 percent of patients with *"lasting deterioration* directly attributable to therapy"* (italics in original, p. 284).

Given the mass of scientific evidence questioning the usefulness of professionals offering insight psychotherapies to patients, why do they continue to do so? Perhaps one kind of insight therapy is better than the others. Wood cites the summarized investigation of nearly four hundred psychotherapy studies, which found

DAVID K. REYNOLDS

no significant differences in results among the lot. Wood concludes, "If, for some reason, you have decided to embark on a course of talk therapy and are worried about which type to invest in, your worries may cease. You can make your selection with a blindfold and a pin" (p. 288). Furthermore, studies indicate that the amount of time spent in talking psychotherapies is unrelated to results.

Although Wood's attack on insight therapies is well conducted and devastating, there is some confusion in the alternative he offers. We agree that it is through sensible attitudes and sometimes difficult action that change must take place, but Wood seems obsessed with reducing guilt and building self-esteem through sytematically taking the more difficult course of action whenever given a choice. Constructive living would argue that low self-esteem, like guilt, provides useful information to us. The doing of life well is rewarding in itself whatever happens to feelings of self-esteem and guilt. One need not always choose a difficult course; rather, one must choose the proper course, difficult or not. If I always chose the difficult course when using this word processor, the manuscript would be long delayed, at best. Wood writes like many Westerners, as though we powerful humans are operating on a relatively passive reality. I prefer to think of reality as presenting us with situations and our cooperating with reality in accomplishing reality's/our purpose. I wish to give our circumstances more of a place in our action-in-the-world and our feelings less a place of prominence than Wood seems to be doing.

OVERSIMPLIFICATION

Defensive oversimplification is a concept long used by Takehisa Kora to describe a kind of neurotic thinking. If only she would come back to me, my life would be fine; If only I could overcome my fear of speaking in public, my life would be perfect; My bad temper is my only real problem are examples of defensive oversimplification. The mistaken thought is that if some single particular problem were to be eliminated, then life would become rosy. Of course, life brings a myriad of problems and satisfactions. Solving one makes us aware of another, and so on.

I wish here to extend the notion of defensive oversimplification to the thinking of some psychotherapists. The complexity of reality is hidden behind single terms such as *addictive personality* and *anorexia nervosa*. If only the release of opioids could be blocked by some medication, the alcoholism or drug addiction or eating disorder could be cured. If only the childhood traumas could be worked through, if only the past learning errors could be corrected, if only the self-esteem could be heightened—all are gross examples of oversimplification.

Reality sends a variety of challenges that cannot be handled with any single tactic of coping.

MORITA ON PSYCHOANALYSIS

Psychoanalysis was just beginning to bloom in the West when Morita developed his understanding and treatment of neurosis. Although psychoanalysis never made much headway in Japan, there were some classic debates between Morita and the leading Japanese psychoanalyst of his time. I have garnered here a few of Morita's considerations on the subject of psychoanalysis, translated from his writings in *Seishin Ryoho Kogi*. Relevant page numbers are in parentheses.

Morita wasn't impressed by the notion of the unconscious. In fact, Freud's definition of the unconscious seemed much too small to Morita. If the unconscious is that which is outside of our awareness, then much more of our living than Freud supposed is carried out by our unconscious. Our blood flow, our heartbeat (192), and temperature regulation are carried out unconsciously. Rather than use the unconscious as an explanation of neurosis, Morita saw lack of awareness (or misfocus of awareness) as the definition of neurosis itself (192). Of course, we aren't aware of the cause of our neurotic moments, because the awareness itself would elimi-

DAVID K. REYNOLDS

nate that moment's neurosis. Reality naturally stimulates the flow of thoughts. Thoughts that aren't relevant to this moment's reality are forgotten (or repressed, if you like) until some reality stimulus calls them out again. Morita saw no need for an elaborate theory of repression (195). When the thoughts are again related to what we experience in this moment's reality, then they pop into awareness (193). For example, we forget writing when we are digging in the garden and then we forget about digging in the garden when we sit down to write (194).

Morita makes no attempt to explain why and in what way these thoughts are related to reality—i.e., why our mind selects these particular thoughts as related to this particular reality. He was clearly less ambitious than Freud in his theorizing. Morita took both reality and thoughts as natural givens. Ambitious theorizing doesn't always provide satisfactory explanation, as the theories of psychoanalysis have demonstrated.

Morita argued that repression can't be the cause of our suffering. Sometimes we can't forget, even when we want to forget. We can't suppress painful or obsessive thoughts at will (194). Forgetting through the natural flow of the mind in accord with the flow of reality would be healthy from Morita's point of view. Clearly, Morita looked at the unconscious as nonawareness in a naturalistic sense, not as the sort of reified psychologic concept put forth by psychoanalytic theory.

Morita pointed out that nearly everyone has childhood experiences that Freudians might point to as the cause of neurosis. But some people remember these experiences, ruminate on them, feel guilt and other unpleasant feelings about them, and so are (not become) neurotic. Why doesn't everyone become neurotic? There must be some character differences among people, Morita supposed (196), based on child-rearing and physiological differences. Constructive-living theory suggests that these character differences proposed by Morita are as ephemeral as the repressed traumas of psychoanalysis in explaining neurotic moments. Why aren't neurotic people always neurotic? Rather than trying to explain the sources of neurosis, it is possible to take them as given and work on living constructively in spite of them.

Psychoanalytic notions that feelings should be recognized, brought into awareness, fits with Morita's thought. But Morita noted that simply expressing feelings doesn't solve our problems (197). In fact, expressing a feeling may actually increase its force (199) rather than discharging its energy, as psychoanalytic theory supposes. When we express anger, for example, the reactions of those who are the targets of our expression may react in a way to escalate our anger (199). Reality provides us with feedback on the degrees of usefulness of expressing feelings from situation to situation.

DAVID K. REYNOLDS

Training for Constructive Living • • •
•   •   •   •   •

WHO IS TRAINED?

We use the following screening questions in making our decision to allow an individual into the ten-day certification program:

1. Have you ever been treated by a psychologist, psychiatrist, or other psychotherapist? For what (diagnosis)? When? What kind of treatment?
2. Have you ever been on medication for mental or nervous difficulties? When? What kind of medication? What was your diagnosis? Are you taking medication now?
3. Have you ever been hospitalized in a psychiatric facility?
4. Have you ever threatened or attempted suicide?
5. Have you ever threatened or attempted homicide?
6. Have you ever been in psychoanalysis? When?
7. Are you undergoing any psychotherapy at this time?
8. Are you in reasonably good mental and physical health at this time?
9. Do you have any dietary or exercise restrictions at this time?
10. Do you take recreational drugs or alcohol? Did you ever?

Both mental-health professionals and nonprofessionals take the training. Mental-health professionals then incorporate the constructive-living methods in their practice and in their personal lives. Nonprofessionals use the methods to give advice to friends, neighbors, and families and in their personal lives. Mental-health professionals have more experience dealing with psychological problems, but they must unlearn and relearn some useless and outdated concepts from their traditional training. Morita wrote that a therapist needs to exhibit both warm maternal love and strict fatherly love (*Seishin Ryoho Kogi*, p. 216). Constructive living teaches the practice (doing) of maternal love through Naikan and the practice of fatherly love through Morita therapy.

PRACTICALITIES OF TRAINING

In the United States, certification training in constructive living costs more than $1,200 for the ten days. Texts, room and board, and travel expenses are additional. Training has been held in Los Angeles, Hawaii, San Francisco, New York, Washington, D.C., and Miami. Shorter workshops (noncertification workshops) have been held in many states and in Tokyo.

Training in the West follows what is called the *iemoto* system in Japan. I certify the constructive-living instructors after they have completed an intensive ten-day course of training and I am confident that they understand and apply constructive-living principles in their daily living. The training course takes place in a setting where the trainees live together, and it continues from morning until night each day with no time out. The morning schedule is as follows: Arise, prepare breakfast together, attend a three-hour morning seminar. In the afternoon, we prepare and eat lunch, clean up, and each trainee has an individual instruction session with an instructor. In the evening we prepare dinner together, eat, and clean up. The rest of the time in the afternoon and evening is devoted to carrying out individual and group constructive-living assignments, including reading, writing letters of thanks, cleaning trash from the neighborhood, attending to sights, sounds, touch, smells, and tastes, and the like.

Midterm and final examinations are part of the course work, as they are in many other educational settings. Those who pass the examinations and demonstrate by their daily lives that they have begun to successfully incorporate constructive-living wisdom into their everyday lives are certified. They receive a life koan, which can be used to further deepen their understanding of this lifeway.

It is important to emphasize that not all who attend and finish the certification-training courses are actually certified. For those who pass the examinations and nevertheless aren't certified there is no need to take the course or the examinations again. They are invited to write to me at least a couple of years later, explaining their understanding of why they weren't certified and how they have changed in such a way as to have now earned certification. That is their life koan.

RULES

In the training, we begin with strict rules assigning serving others at meals, for example, or restricting speech. Then the rules are relaxed and trainees are asked to maintain the spirit of the rules on a voluntary basis. Then the students are encouraged to simply continue living according to the principles from which the rules emerged.

In the same manner, assignments are given by the instructors at first, then the trainees are encouraged to create their own assignments and exercises for themselves.

POWER TRIP

New instructors in constructive living may be seduced by concerns of power. Unless they have a firm grounding in the Naikan side of constructive living, they may relish the authority of making assignments, giving exercises to the unenlightened student. Furthermore, they may be concerned that their authority over the student's life may cause some irreparable psychological damage if the wrong assignment is made.

Both of these problems come from a fundamental misunderstanding in the authority in constructive living. The instructor is merely a guide, freely offering suggestions on the basis of his or her experience. The student, in similar fashion, is free to listen or not, try out a suggestion or not, return for more instruction or not. The instructor is far less important in the student's life than either the instructor or the student may think. Remember, the real teacher of constructive living is reality itself.

Contemplation and Commentary

In this chapter we'll consider some of Morita's ideas and their meaning in the modern world. The first reflections come from Morita's book *Seishin Ryoho Kogi*. The numbers in parentheses are page numbers from the 1983 Hakuyosha reprint of the book published originally in 1921.

ACTIVITY

Morita pointed out that physical exercise not only trains the body but trains the mind as well (44). Remember that Morita considered the mind and body as manifestations of the same mind-body whole. A regular program of exercise continued over time develops discipline and endurance.

Morita approved of competitive sports and games. They encourage the participants to put out effort and courageous behavior. They build sociability and harmony and cooperation (145). But he emphasized that activities should be purposeful. Morita preferred shopping and hikes for the purpose of collecting things rather than aimless strolling (146).

All this activity, however, must be balanced by rest, good

nutrition, and quiet support from others. Morita noted that socializing with extroverted people may tire some neurotics, and socializing with other neurotics may lead to destructive complaining (147).

In general, Morita didn't prescribe vacations for his students. He found it more useful to send them to work or to school. Their low self-esteem came from failure to live up to their own expectations and their awareness of their own irresponsibility (147). Flight into vacations or a series of rapid job changes only made their difficulties worse. People who are unemployed by circumstances beyond their control can do what needs doing around the home and in the garden and in church and other volunteer activities while actively seeking to find employment.

PURPOSE

However, it is important to keep clear on our purposes when engaging in any pursuit. For example, money is needed for our housing, clothing, food. Sometimes those purposes are forgotten and we may become immersed in accumulating money as an end in itself. We become distracted from important purposes (149–150).

Morita pointed out that all work isn't fun. But it may be necessary to achieve our purposes. And we must attend to the work before us, putting forth effortful action anyway (167).

FORGETTING

Concentrating on having good health is unnatural, Morita held. When we have good health, we ignore it (168). Of course, that is not to say that we can ignore good health practices in our lives. Rather, when our lives become oriented toward healthy living with sound habits, our attention turns naturally to the cues from reality about what needs doing. People who fill their minds with narrow thoughts about the current health fads may be distracting themselves from broader teachings from reality. When the gloves fit well, we

DAVID K. REYNOLDS

forget them. When the car drives well, we forget it. When our bodies function well, we don't pay particular attention to them.

In fact, forgetting is an important part of the overcoming of neurotic tendencies. Morita noticed that when parents must invest themselves in the care of a seriously ill child, they may be cured of their neuroses (202). They become so absorbed in the treatment of their child that they forget themselves, they forget their neurotic complaints.

SUGGESTION

When we hear others yawn or clear their throats and we want to do the same, that is one form of suggestion (178). We are influenced by suggestion often in our daily lives. In fact, suggestion helps society operate with relative smoothness.

In teaching a constructive lifeway (or in therapy), however, suggestion has some disadvantages. Morita pointed out that suggestion reduces the student's ability to make his/her own judgments (182). As always, Morita wanted his students to be able to respond appropriately to the changing circumstances that reality brings them. Suggestion narrows the student's focus. Advice comes from the instructor. The student merely waits for the advice and obeys. To some degree, suggestion cannot altogether be avoided, particularly in the beginning of training. However, humor and reverse role-playing and questioning by the instructor can reduce the effects of suggestion as instruction proceeds.

Another disadvantage of suggestion is that its effectiveness in reducing suffering and increasing the likelihood of effortful and purposeful behavior varies from student to student and from time to time (211). There is lots of reality to which the student may respond beyond the suggestion from the instructor. Reality remains the teacher worth attention and emulation.

The following set of observations come from the book *The Path to Self-Knowledge and Realization (Jikaku to Satori he no Michi)*, written by Morita and journalist Mizutani Keiji. Page numbers are from the Hakuyosha edition of the book republished in 1959.

CIRCUMSTANCES

The strength of desires tends to decrease with a long illness (177) and with sorrow (149).

Morita pointed out that he neither liked nor disliked going to the market to buy apples. If he felt bored, it wasn't so onerous. If asked by his teacher, then he would happily do it because there was a debt to repay and he wanted to be liked by the teacher. Circumstances determine our likes and dislikes (179).

We pick shells at the beach, then throw them away after coming home because we become bored with them and there is a variety of objects at home to attract our attention. And some patients in hospitals don't notice the beautiful plants around their beds because they are thinking only of what will work to cure them instead of keeping their eyes open and letting the natural mind work (150).

THE NATURAL MIND

We don't have to work to create a natural mind; it just is (58). You don't have to make an empty stomach feel hungry (174). When a bird flies up at your feet you feel startled, naturally (210). Trying to tame or control the natural mind is a mistake. Some students, for example, understand that alcohol isn't good for their health. Then they try to make their natural minds not want to drink the alcohol. They must learn, advised Morita, to accept the subjective reality that they want to drink alcohol along with the objective reality that it will harm them. Both are true (202). Control comes in the area of behavior.

Morita recommended that we worry when we worry, that we be cold when it's cold. When we are hot (e.g., when we have a fever) and it's cold, then there is some unnatural problem (171).

DAVID K. REYNOLDS

Some therapists will try to get patients to stop worrying and relax. Such is not a goal of Morita's way (171).

The step from the natural mind to the neurotic mind is exemplified by those with compulsive cleanliness disorders. They begin with the natural purpose of wanting to be clean and live in clean surroundings to the distorted purpose of wanting to avoid feelings of uncleanliness (145). They move from the relatively controllable to the uncontrollable.

CURE

Cure of neurosis has a special meaning in constructive living. Morita suggested that his students might give up but keep on climbing the mountain (160).

If we watch and emulate others who seem to be doing well, then we are on the path to cure. If we think that we are different from everyone else and special in our own neurotic way and then complain about this distinctiveness, we aren't on the path to improvement (189). It isn't necessary to stop thinking imaginatively and intellectually; it is necessary, however, to stop talking so much and quietly observe our surroundings (197). The introspective ability of the *shinkeishitsu* neurotic can help maintain a balance in life. The best scholars, teachers, and religious leaders have been *shinkeishitsu* (184).

In order to improve ourselves, we must study ourselves. If we have no desire to study ourselves, even if someone explains the principles to us we won't understand (210). When we begin to be interested in the circumstances that generate anger in us, then we begin to study and learn. When we ought to be angry, we are angry (210). I might add that an infant's first emotional responses are to reality. As we grow older, we start responding to imagination and memories and word-generated reality as well.

Part of the process of cure is learning to bear initial discomfort. During surgery, most of the experience of pain comes from the cutting of skin, not from cutting the deeper areas of the body.

When getting into a hot bath, the initial discomfort passes with time (192). It is important to endure while remaining mindful of one's goals.

Morita noticed that among the *shinkeishitsu* neurotics he treated, those who achieved "cure" caught fewer colds (he suspected increased natural resistance). They were able to go to sleep immediately, to awaken early feeling well rested. They were more efficient in their lives and maintained an improved life view (181).

Morita noticed that some students were cured of their insomnia and anxiety attacks and a variety of other complaints merely by reading his books and practicing the natural life canons (144). I can vouch for that observation. Hundreds of readers of our books about constructive living have kindly taken the trouble to write about improvements in their lives from practicing the constructive-living methods.

ON DEATH

Morita believed that there is no universally understandable content to words describing an afterlife, or good fortune, or even what it is to be "a fine fellow." We invest such words with private meaning based on our life experience, education, and so forth (169). For Morita, eternal life meant writing and teaching (169). I suspect that he did not mean only the results of writing and teaching, but the process itself was already eternal life. Have you ever lost yourself in eternity doing some tasks? Great men may have needs and desires greater than their fear of death, but all fear death (179).

The opposite of joy is sorrow, Morita pointed out; the opposite of life is death. It's like moving a teacup from here to there (172).

DAVID K. REYNOLDS

On Naikan

This chapter is based on a keynote lecture presented at the Twelfth National Naikan Meetings held in Toyama, Japan, on May 28, 1989.

OKAGESAMADE

When I first went to Japan, I heard people replying to the greeting "How are you?" with the reply "*Okagesama de . . .*" or "Thanks to you . . ." I couldn't understand how one's own health should be thanks to some other person. Even when people inquired about the health of my mother, a person they had never met, I was taught to reply, "She's quite well, thanks to you." It seemed very strange to me.

I'm sure that some Japanese use this form of greeting without thinking, just as some Americans would automatically answer the question "How are you?" with "I'm fine," even when they don't feel fine. But there is some special truth about *Okagesama* that I discovered thanks to a process of looking at reality called Naikan.

I plan to present to you the case for the notion that anyone who looks carefully and straightforwardly at reality will necessarily come up with a response of gratitude. I shall argue that it takes energy and effort to ignore the realistic contributions of others to our lives. In other words, we can only keep gratitude and the desire to repay others out of our minds by walking about blindly with our eyes closed to the myriads of concrete and specific instances of the supporting care of others in our lives.

The idea that nobody ever cared about me or nobody ever understood me is based on self-centeredness and stupidity. The phrase *Okagesama de* seems quite natural and proper to me now. Let's investigate the thinking that led to this change in my thinking.

CONSTRUCTIVE LIVING

In the West, we practice an extension of Naikan and Morita therapy called constructive living. The methods of Yoshimoto and Morita have been adapted to meet the needs of Westerners. That adaptation was made possible by the depth of thought and the common human elements of Morita and Naikan practices. Our constructive living has already had some influence on the practice of Morita therapy in Japan. You will find some Naikan-like elements in Morita therapy in Japan today. Before Yoshimoto Sensei died, it was my pleasure to introduce to him several of the leaders of Morita therapy in Japan and of constructive living in the West.

First, I must say that the heart of Naikan is action/behavior, not thinking or feeling. In classic form, the Naikan therapist moves from client to client, bowing, listening to the client's report, offering advice when necessary, serving food, preserving the opportunity for the Naikansha to reflect on the Naikan themes. These actions by the Naikan guide are models of service for the Naikansha.

Whatever the Naikansha recall, no matter how moved they are by their self-reflection, if their Naikan isn't reflected in their words to the guide, in the eating of their food and their bathing and dressing and laying out of their bedding, if their actions when they leave the Naikan setting aren't changed in ways that reflect service to people and proper use of objects and energy in the world, then they haven't done proper Naikan.

70

There are dangers in too much emphasis on the emotional aspects of Naikan. There are hazards in too much talk about gratitude and guilt and other feelings that accompany Naikan. There are risks when there is too much concern with changed attitudes and inspiration and mystical experiences. Of course, these changes in the psyche may occur during Naikan. But they are ephemeral and uncontrollable directly by the will. We cannot make ourselves feel grateful or guilty or desiring to serve others directly by our will or directly by means of any other technique. Even when we do Naikan, the feelings come and go in some rhythm and pace that we cannot dictate or even understand.

What I am saying is that feelings—however striking they may be in our experience and observation of Naikan—are not satisfactorily solid bases for building a lifeway or a therapy. Only by changed behavior can we feel certain about evaluating the success or depth of Naikan. As you may know. Yoshimoto Sensei and his staff used to assign numerical evaluations of Naikan depth to Naikansha at the Nara Naikan Center. From the beginning, Yoshimoto Sensei realized how difficult it is to evaluate a person's Naikan depth. I would suggest that the reason why evaluation is so difficult is that the sample of behavior one can observe is too small and constrained by the setting to make a judgment of Naikan depth. I would feel more comfortable with an evaluation of Naikan depth based on a person's daily life in the month following intensive Naikan.

A CHANCE TO WIN, EVEN THOUGH WE FAIL

In our practice of Naikan in the United States, we don't ask our students to reflect only on past "lies and stealing," as is sometimes done in Japanese Naikan practice, because there is no chance to win the game, no possible balance as in received-returned. Troubles caused is part of a balance, i.e., the troubles caused us. We are righting the misremembered balance by Naikan. But the theme of lies and stealing is a straightforward attack on the self.

I believe that the power of Naikan lies in the chance of winning, the chance of finding a balance, and the practical impossibility of it. We can evaluate ourselves by our own standards with the chance of finding some balance, but we always, inevitably, come up short. The contrast between the possibility and the actuality creates the dynamic tension of Naikan.

THE ORDER OF NAIKAN

In our constructive-living training, we begin Naikan on the mother or mother surrogate just as is done in Japan. We move from family members to other people whose names we know. Then we begin daily Naikan on people whose names we don't know but whose faces we have seen (for example, the clerk in the store or the driver who stopped for us at a crosswalk). Next we do daily Naikan on people whose names we don't know and whose faces we have never seen (for example, the carpenter who built the chair we sit on). We move next to other living creatures, both animals and plants. Naikan continues with nonliving objects (what our shoes do for us, for example, and what we have done in return for our shoes, and the troubles we have caused our shoes). Finally, we consider energy (such as electricity) from a Naikan perspective.

One of our constructive-living instructors, Gregg Krech, has devised an exercise for eating special Naikan meals. We make a list of twenty or thirty or more people who have contributed to the meal we are about to eat. Then we begin at the top of the list and reflect on the contribution of that person to our meal as we eat the first bite. We reflect on the second person on the list with our second bite of food. And so on.

REALISTIC NAIKAN

Naikan is not about inside or outside; it is not about beautiful or ugly. It is about reality. Naikan isn't wonderful because people feel it deeply. It is wonderful because it is about reality, about truth. Feelings change; truth doesn't.

During the Naikan conference held in 1988, I took a walk

DAVID K. REYNOLDS

early in the morning down the hill to the local cemetery. Little blue wildflowers were blooming there. Artificial flowers, too, were placed on the graves. Artificial flowers are pretty and take little maintenance. But they aren't real. Beware of zoka (artificial flower) Naikan.

At that Naikan conference in 1988, one presenter talked about a girl who came to see her mother as a lonely and unappreciated human. She came to see reality. In other words, she was freed from her misperceptions (mayotta ninshiki) to see the reality of her mother as a human with needs, frustrations, and pain, too, like the girl herself. She was no longer so bound by the false image created by her mind.

Some Americans, when they first come to practice Naikan, mistakenly believe that Naikan aims at turning their memories of parents from all bad to all good. But Naikan aims at presenting nothing more or less than reality, at turning cardboard paper-doll images of parents into more rounded, realistic images.

NEW LIVES FOR PEOPLE AND THINGS

In a book titled *The Path Toward Awakening and Enlightenment (Jikaku to Satori he no Michi)*, Morita Masatake (a Japanese psychiatrist and contemporary of Freud) and his associate Mizutani Keiji set forth some advice about the proper use of ourselves and our surroundings. One result of understanding these writings is the realization that the proper use of ourselves *is* the proper use of our surroundings, and vice versa. The two are not different. I offer here an interpretation and elaboration of some of the contents of this stimulating book.

Morita's advice to those who held grudges against their parents was to work on themselves, not their parents. At first glance, his suggestions seem alien and difficult to understand for Westerners. "Look for the faults within yourself that made you unlovable; then go apologize to your father and mother." "Abandon your resistance to your parents." "Stop the fighting unilaterally and begin serving them." What a strange prescription to read in these modern times!

Certainly, it is easy to dismiss such advice on the grounds that times have changed and that Japanese culture is different from Euro-American culture. Calling his counsel culture-bound is a convenient way to avoid looking at the deeper, human wisdom within which it is framed. There are few who see the difficulties and sacrifices of parenthood until they become parents themselves. Morita noted that one young man recognized the love of his parents only after overcoming his neurotic life-style. Our own misery and self-centeredness interfere with our ability to see our parents' and others' efforts in our behalf.

Our sacrifices for others, when such offerings occur, are too often gauged to achieve some self-serving purpose—to be liked, for example, or to be appreciated, respected, rewarded. Now, Morita isn't going to give the expected pretentious advice to "straighten up and fly right." And he's not going to recommend that we work on our confidence and self-image in order to develop motivation and strength to improve. He suggests that we say to ourselves something like this: "I'm a difficult person to live with. I want things to go my own way, but it just isn't right to act with my own convenience in mind all the time. I'm going to be disliked by people some of the time whatever I do. But I shall act for others' benefit some of the time just because that is the natural and proper thing to do." Such an attitude, said Morita, is the basis of religion. It's not necessary to invoke God or love of humanity as the reason for serving others; it is enough to recognize that the desire to serve others comes from the unremarkable, natural mind.

As noted briefly above, no matter what we do there will be some times when some people dislike us. We can reduce the likelihood of encountering dislike by our actions, but we can never eliminate it. Some people are forever apologizing while continuing the habits that alienate others. "To ask 'Don't think badly of me' while doing something disagreeable is foolishness," Morita pointed out.

As pointed out above, Naikan is a modern secular method for examining our debt to the world and our progress in repaying that debt. Historically derived from Shinshu Buddhism in Japan, Naikan was created and modified by Yoshimoto Ishin. The founder of Shinshu Buddhism was a historical figure named Shinran. Morita Masatake saw his own thinking to be similar to that of Shinran in some regards. Both Shinran and Morita considered doubting to be natural and appropriate to human life. Great Zen Buddhist thinkers, too, considered great doubt necessary to achieving great enlightenment. Doubting the reasonableness of these insights or doubting the usefulness of constructive living is quite all right. Like Morita, we recommend that while doubting you give this lifeway a try and observe the results.

Morita's approach to life impels us to use the objects and energies around us with care. Morita suggested that we use our lives and the things in our lives well, that we find novel uses for and give new lives to things and people. His care with the use of water (for washing, then mopping, then plants) and scrap wood (for heating the bath) and even the discarded vegetables at the local grocer's (as feed for domestic animals) is legendary. But Morita wasn't merely concerned with saving money. He was engaged in discovering and exercising the proper use of those objects. In the same fashion, he discovered and exercised the proper use of himself. It is said that when he bought some bamboo poles, the shopkeeper offered to deliver them. But Morita, the elite professor, was heading home anyway, so he carried the bamboo poles himself. Why use the delivery person's energy (even though it is free) when the task could be accomplished more efficiently by Morita himself?

Finally, Morita offered the following advice about advice. It is as applicable here as elsewhere. He recommended that we thank others when they offer advice, even if the advice is poor, but we have no obligation to like it or to adopt it.

In *The Gift* (New York: Vintage, 1979), Lewis Hyde offers some stimulating thoughts about giving and receiving. He holds that gifts, whether they be material goods or talents, must be passed along. The gifts themselves or something of comparable value must be given away. The gifts then create a social bond between givers and recipients. To fail to pass on a gift ruins the gift and the person who hoards it, and subsequent social ties are weakened. Naikan would suggest that we all fail to keep the gifts moving.

One major difference between Hyde's position and Yoshimoto's position has to do with the market model. Hyde doesn't approve of the market equilibrium model. Rather than reaching balance between giving and receiving, he wishes to see an unbalanced momentum of gifts being passed along from person to person, like a tumbling row of dominoes. Hyde believes that an exchange model doesn't allow the human contact of gift giving. Exchange is too calculating. I think that the Naikan position would be that although the exchange model seeks balance, there is in fact no balance achieved in the real world.

Hyde argues that gratitude is the feeling we experience between the time we receive a gift and the time we give it away again. And it is the gratitude we feel that prompts us to pass along the gift. We may feel some generalized residue of gratitude after we give away a gift, however. I suspect that Hyde considers gifts in a much narrower sense than did Yoshimoto. From the Naikan perspective, the gifts are so pervasive and overwhelming that we don't even recognize or keep them in mind all the time, much less repay them as we receive them.

Hyde does make an observation that I think is important for Naikan, particularly for Naikan in Japan. He notices that when giving or returning a gift involves calculation and obligation, it is no longer gift giving. I think that the obligations involved in Japanese gift exchanges have both positive and negative aspects. On the one hand, being obligated to give or return a gift more or less ensures that balances are maintained in Japan. Westerners, acting

DAVID K. REYNOLDS

on feelings of gratitude, may fail to bring or return gifts when not in the mood. On the other hand, the attitude behind the gift in Japan may be one of annoyance, burden, obligation. Of course, one is never sure of the feelings behind a gift in any country. And one may well opt for the concrete gift rather than some ephemeral feeling that might lie behind the gift. Nevertheless, even when one wishes to give a gift in Japan, there is the shadow of "must" behind it.

Naikan does ask the Naikan student to reflect on the attitudes with which gifts were received and returned. Still, there is sometimes the strong sense of debts owed that makes the giving no longer an expression of gratitude. It can be argued that attempting to pay our debts is as important as giving gifts to others. Still, paying off a debt seems to come from dark poverty, while giving a gift seems to come from bright plenty.

Hyde believes that differentiating and calculating the gifts we have received and returned, as one does during Naikan reflection, somehow reduces gift giving to logical market exchange thinking. He supposes that it pulls the gift out of the realm of bestowal into the realm of commerce. I'm not so sure. Perhaps only after we take a clear, itemized reckoning of the gifts we have received are we ready and willing to give the gifts others merit.

In the end Hyde comments that "The great materialists . . . are those who have extended the commodity form of value into the human body, while the great spiritual figures, like the Buddha, are those who have used their own bodies to extend the worth of gifts just as far." If there was any recent example of a person who used his body to extend the worth of gifts it was Yoshimoto Sensei. I won't forget the image of his dragging his body along the tatami mats from byobu screen to byobu screen during Naikan interviews because raising up on those painful knees was so difficult.

WHAT NAIKAN IS NOT

Some people seem to think that Naikan is about forgiving others for the harm they caused us in the past. But Naikan is much more deeply gashing than that minor scratch of forgiveness and tolerance. Its depth comes from discovering the wonder that others have been able to forgive and tolerate us, that we have hurt those very people we accuse of hurting us.

Charlie came to my office to tell me about his Naikan-based progress in dealing with his mother.

"After I sent that letter thanking my mother for what she had given me, she called to thank me."

"Did that surprise you?"

"Not really. She also reminded me of money she had spent on me in the past that wasn't included in my letter. But that was all right. I somehow had the sense that she had done the best she knew how in raising me. I felt an unexpected, peaceful feeling about her. It was interesting to see that the things she used to do to upset me no longer have much effect on me. I see her more clearly. I realize now that when she is controlling and negative and vicious, it is the way she learned to survive. She's not aiming all that negativity just at me. It's just the way she is, especially with her family. I now can feel some gratitude for what she did for me."

"What has happened since then? Have you had more contact with your mother?"

"Yes. I took her out to dinner a few times. And I've been remembering to say thank you to her as much as I can. The problem I had with her recently was during a weekend of holiday shopping we did together. She kept trying to control me and kept attacking me. I kept on giving to her in spite of her harsh attitude, even though I felt awfully tense for most of the time we were together. Maybe we just can't spend that much time together. I guess the closeness is too scary for her. As long as she stays across town and we talk on the phone now and then, it's okay.

"Who knows, maybe one day her vicious ways won't bother me at all even if we are together for a long time. She really doesn't mean to be so malicious."

"I see you are making real effort to adopt a Naikan perspective on your mother. How about a Naikan perspective on yourself?"

DAVID K. REYNOLDS

"I have been using Naikan with other people I felt angry with in the past. Looking at what I ought to be grateful for has helped me let go of some of the bitterness I felt. I feel more open and connected to others now. Before I go to sleep at night, I think of the things I can be grateful for during the day."

"Thank you for your struggle with this Naikan venture. I wonder—"

"I want to thank *you*. I have been dedicated to my own growth for many years now. You have helped me become a better person."

Charlie is just beginning on the path of Naikan self-reflection. As can be seen from the above conversation, he wanders into the bushes on right and left. I wish him the best in his journey.

There are key phrases that flash alarms in my mind when they are uttered during Naikan interviews. "She would . . ."; "she used to . . ."; "she always . . ."; "she never . . ."; "I'm grateful for all the . . . she . . ."; "I received a lot of . . ."; "thank you for the many things . . ." are examples of such phrases. They allow the Naikan student to escape from looking at concrete, specific favors received from others in the past. They offer the escape routes of generalization and dismissal. Recalling specific events and services rendered by others will have much more impact on the student.

Some students go to great lengths to avoid doing genuine Naikan. One student related the following incidents he classified as favors he did for his father: "I didn't complain as my father drove me to the hospital for stitches after I gashed my knee, and when I wrecked the car Dad gave me, I paid for the repair of the damages myself."

WORDS OF THANKS

There is merit in developing a variety of ways to thank others. Listen for the occasions and ways in which others say thanks. Develop a repertoire of words of appreciation. The same old thank you becomes tiring to the listener and the speaker when repeated without variation. Mix it up with words like *grateful, appreciate, kind, thoughtful, generous, considerate,* and *unselfish.* Change the inflection of your voice so that the same words of gratitude sound different in different circumstances.

As always, there need not be feelings of gratitude when the words are uttered. Feelings cannot be generated on demand with any consistency. But another's act of kindness (even another's words of appreciation) merit the words of thanks whether one truly feels grateful or not. In the speaking of thanks sometimes feelings of appreciation emerge. In any case, the words are due those who support us in some way.

One proper response to "Thank you" is "Thank you."

DIFFICULT NAIKAN

Some Naikan topics are more difficult than others. Some parents, while nurturing and supporting their children, did also hurt their children in terrible ways. The children of such parents have a marvelous opportunity to do deep Naikan. If they can spot little green plants in the tiny crevices of a huge, cold gray cliff, then they can spot green anywhere. Difficult Naikan is still worth doing well.

What is the value in having groups for children of alcoholic parents aimed at finding the many ways in which parents hurt their children? What good does it do to explore the tragedies of mistreatment and then fail to go beyond insight to constructive action? Discovering both positive and negative sides of past reality will lead to a more balanced perspective on one's present existence, too. To use computer terms, we recommend that our students upgrade their memory with Naikan.

PART II

PEOPLE: MOTHER, MORITA, MRS.P, AND ME

In this section are some personal vignettes I wish to offer you. They are about people who are connected with constructive living.

The first chapter is about my mother and some of the lessons she teaches with her life. The second chapter is about the life of Morita. Little is yet written about Morita Masatake the man, in English. The third chapter contains excerpts from a letter written by a woman who suffers from rheumatoid arthritis and uses constructive living in her daily life. And the final chapter in this section is about my life; although, of course, it can be said that much of this book is on the same subject.

Mother Tales

Not too long ago, I wrote on a Mother's Day card that knowing Mom made me look forward to becoming old. Here's why.

Mom says she is too young for a computer yet. She wants to be as physically active as she can be until her age and physical condition limit her mobility. Then she'll sit down in front of a monitor and master personal computing.

I am sometimes shy and reluctant to speak up. When Mom enters a store, she is likely to march up to the nearest clerk and inquire whether the store offers a discount for senior citizens. I can remember my father ordering a cup of coffee and paying for it even though the waitress forgot to bring it. Not Mom. When service is bad or slow, when goods are inferior or marred, Mom speaks up.

Since Dad died, there have been many men eager to spend an evening in dinner and conversation with Mom. She could eat out every night of the week if she wished. Although in her seventies, she looks, acts, and feels like she is in her fifties. Her male friends, most of them in their fifties, never suspect her true age. And she isn't about to tell them.

There are times, however, when Mom is tired and wants to be

alone. Then she hangs a DO NOT DISTURB sign on her door and refuses to open it or answer the telephone until she is quite ready to be her charming social self again.

Recently, at seventy-five, she passed the test for obtaining a driver's license. And she bought a car for getting around in Oregon. But she uses a friend's car and the municipal bus system to travel around when in Los Angeles. Once her purse was slit by a pickpocket on the bus. I would have seriously considered riding a different bus line, but Mom continued to ride the same bus line with the same purse. This time, however, it was filled with pins and razor blades. Sometimes on the crowded bus she would hear cries of pain from unsuspecting fellows who reached inside her trap.

Mom drinks several cups of coffee each morning with some sort of pastry. She walks an hour or two every day, and sometimes more. Until very recently, her legs held out longer while shopping than mine, although I claim that is because shopping holds her interest longer than mine so she just doesn't notice the tiredness in her legs.

Mom worked as a secretary while my sister and I were growing up. She came home from work and produced quick, tasty meals. She passed on her love of cooking and her dislike of dishwashing to me. Mom was always ready to listen, always trusting of my judgment, always offering freedom for others' growth. She was constantly turning our attention to reality—during long trips in the car, she kept her easily bored children alert by pointing out interesting scenes as we passed along.

Mom didn't know the words *constructive living* or the theory underlying it, but she lived and continues to live many of its principles naturally.

My mother isn't "comfortable" flying in airplanes. Nevertheless, she flies when necessary. Several years ago, she visited me in Japan for the first time. On the flight over she enjoyed the movie, a comedy. According to my wife, Mom laughed at the antics of the characters on the screen. It wasn't until after she landed that she

DAVID K. REYNOLDS

learned she didn't have to watch the movie in Korean (a language, like Japanese, Mother doesn't understand at all). A switch in the armrest of her seat would have brought her an English soundtrack. No matter.

In Japan, we went shopping at a large department store. After shopping on the seventh floor, we entered a descending elevator. The elevator operator politely bowed to the passengers and asked in Japanese if anyone wanted to get off at the sixth floor. Her eyes met Mom's. Mom nodded her head and smiled. At the sixth floor the doors opened but no one got out. The elevator operator bowed and asked if anyone wanted to get off at the fifth floor. Her eyes swept the elevator. Again, when their eyes and smiles met, Mom nodded her head. Again the elevator stopped and no one exited.

"Mom, please stop that," I whispered. "She's asking who wants to get off at these floors. When you nod and smile at her she thinks you want to get off."

"No, I'm not requesting a floor," Mother retorted. "That cute girl smiles and nods at me, and I smile and nod back at her. I'm just being polite."

"Mom!"

The game continued. At each floor Mom nodded and smiled. At each floor we stopped and no one exited. I felt increasingly embarrassed at Mother's obstinate behavior. My mind was spinning visions of the trouble we were causing the elevator's passengers and especially the poor operator who, I imagined, would have much preferred to skip right to the ground floor and dump this troublesome Caucasian lady back into the crowds on the street.

I wanted to hide, to pretend I didn't know this character—though we clearly stood out among the elevator's passengers. My mind worked and worked on creating misery for me. At last we arrived at the ground floor. It was my chance to flee from this embarrassing scene. Exiting from the rear of the elevator, we were the last to leave. As Mom passed the young girl, she took advantage of her last chance to nod and smile at her. I winced. Would the operator take advantage of this moment of privacy to scold

Mother for her aggravating behavior? Would she stare in icy silence?

What happened taught me about the neurotic constructions of my mind. In fact, what happened was the elevator operator tittered and waved a cheery greeting back at Mother. Apparently, she had enjoyed the diversion provided by Mom's actions. Far from taking offense, she had delighted in Mom's company! The predicament was only in my mind. Ah yes, reality again . . .

A couple of days later, Mother provided me with another constructive-living insight. She decided she wanted to order a cup of coffee at a McDonald's restaurant in Hamamatsu. She insisted on overcoming the language barrier with no assistance. Her boldness both impresses and distresses me.

Mom approached the counter and spoke clearly, "Coffee."

The clerk understood and countered with "Aisuka, hottoka." The ball was in Mom's court.

Sharp thinking and circumstantial evidence led her to the conclusion that he was asking her if she wanted iced coffee or hot coffee.

"Hot," she replied, keeping things simple.

Now *hot* and *hotto* don't sound all that similar to Japanese ears. The fellow called an associate. They conferred. They decided that, provided this exchange wasn't going way off track, the foreign lady was saying something closer to *hotto* than to *aisu*. So the clerk brought Mom a cup of hot coffee.

Mom said, "Sugar."

There is a Japanese word, *osato,* which means sugar, but the Japanese have adopted the English word, too, in the form of *sugaa.* So the clerk understood Mom immediately and brought a tube filled with sugar, just as she requested. The problem was the container. In the United States, McDonald's serves sugar in a little rectangular packet. In Japan it comes in what looks like half a drinking straw wrapped in paper.

Mom looked at the clerk's offering and assumed he had misunderstood her. Once more, a little louder, "Sugar." The clerk understood and tried to convince Mother that the sugar was right before her eyes in the tube on the counter. Again, louder, *"Sugar."*

Right before her eyes was a perfect cup of coffee, just as she ordered it. But Mother didn't recognize it. I like to tell this story to my students because they may suffer from a similar misunderstanding. Their minds are just fine as they are. There is no need to fix them. The anxiety they feel tells them about what is important to them and how much they want something and fear not getting it. The voices in their minds that criticize them are to be thanked, not extinguished. Those voices won't let them be satisfied with anything but being the best of which they are capable. The guilt tells them about wrongs that need to be righted, behaviors that need to be upgraded. The perfect cup of coffee is there if only they would recognize it.

Mom, just being Mom, had a great time in Japan. I was exhausted after her visit. Yes, the coffee was perfect as it was.

Morita's Life

As the constructive-living movement gains attention, people want to know more about the founder, Morita. What kind of person was he?

Morita Masatake (his given name can also be read Shoma) was born in Fuke village in Kochi prefecture on the island of Shikoku on January 18, 1874. His father was a schoolteacher and minor village official, strong-willed and proud. Morita's mother was filled with curiosity and energy. Two days after her son's birth, she was up and working. In addition to housework, she did cottage-industry piecework and attended classes in the arts and astronomy. She was a progressive woman of her day. She had a nervous temperament and was somewhat hypochondriacal. At age forty-three she was confined to bed with psychosomatic complaints but recovered quickly when a young child with a serious illness required her care.

Morita grew up under the strict hand of his teacher/father. He disliked school, rebelling to the degree that it took seven years to complete the five-year course of middle school. Morita ran away from home at least once. He suffered from various psychosomatic illnesses as a youth, including headaches, stomach trouble, a disorder misdiagnosed as heart disease, and another disorder misdiagnosed as beriberi (a vitamin deficiency found in countries where polished rice is the staple). He wet his bed until he was twelve. As a child he was taken to a local temple. There he saw a mural depicting the tortures of hell—including lakes of fire and mountains of needles. The sensitive Morita was so upset by the possibility of facing such a future after death that he had trouble sleeping. His concern with death and insistence on the proper use of life persisted until his own death in 1938.

From boyhood, Morita had a broad interest in a wide variety of activities. He cared for rabbits, carp, and monkeys. He practiced archery, the music of the samisen, Zen, and Japanese chess. He was intrigued by fortune-telling, legends, and superstitions. He was a popular lad, getting along well with old and young, male and female, of all ranks and occupations. Throughout his life he socially drank a surprising amount of alcohol, given his active lifestyle and body weakened by typhus and other diseases.

Early promise set him on an elite course that took him in 1898 out of the small town in rural Shikoku to urban Tokyo. His early studies at Tokyo Imperial University indicated his growing interest in the human mind. He conducted research in hypnosis, dreams, delusions, and superstitions. A variety of psychosomatic complaints interfered with his studies. He was concerned with headaches, stomach complaints, and a (misdiagnosed) supposed problem with his heart. He tried numerous medicines and other cures with no substantial effect.

For a period during Morita's first year in the university, his father didn't send the expected school allowance, and Morita was forced to visit a pawnshop for the first time in his life. Morita was angry at his father, suspecting that he was being taken lightly or that his father was pressuring him to return home from Tokyo. So the young man decided to quit taking medicine and literally study himself to death. Then his parents would regret their actions. He immersed himself in studies without taking particular care of his body. The results were that his psychosomatic, neurasthenic symptoms disappeared; furthermore, his grades improved. There is no doubt that this experience had a profound effect on the development of Morita's thinking on the treatment of neurosis.

By 1903, at age twenty-nine, he was lecturing at Jikei University, where he would become professor and chairman of the department of psychiatry and neurology. In 1919, he opened his home to treat neurotic people. That year he worked with eighteen patients in this family setting. He acknowledged the importance of his wife's assistance in this unusual practice outside a hospital or clinic. At first he charged nothing more than expenses for room and board. Many stories come down from those days.

Morita went out with his patients/students to collect the discarded vegetables from the local grocer to feed the pets. Similarly, they collected discarded wood to burn for heating the bath. It was not that Morita was miserly. As noted in an earlier section, his concern was with using things properly, fully, without waste.

In 1920 Morita suffered a near-fatal illness. It provoked soul-searching and a commitment to a life work. After that time, his activities seemed more focused.

He continued to teach at the university. His books ranged from academic texts to best-sellers. He was a popular lecturer and a charming therapist. There were times when he scolded others severely, and even a few times when he hit them. He reported in his diary that he did not do so as a therapeutic technique or in order to shock his students. Rather, he was just deeply involved in their progress and the result emerged naturally from the situation. In that era such behavior was not exceptional, and the results were felicitous.

Perhaps it was the year 1925 in which we can find the full flowering of Morita's method. One night he couldn't sleep well. At around three o'clock in the morning Morita arose and began writing. He wrote that neurosis is not an illness. The more one tries to cure the obsessive problem, the more one becomes obsessed by it. This characteristic perspective tied together what Morita had been doing for a number of years.

Morita's only son died after a long illness at age twenty, in 1930. Then Morita's wife died in 1935. Morita was confined to bed with high fever on occasion during the last three years of his life. He gauged his activity on the basis of an objective measure of his health, his temperature. Active work in the garden alongside his students, a walk, or writing were possible when his strength and temperature permitted. When it began to rise he would read, when it rose higher he would have someone read to him.

Near the end, Morita's breathing was sometimes difficult. He carefully described the progress of his disease to his medical students, using even his dying as a tool of teaching. He was fearful of dying, and that fear was natural and acceptable to Morita. He remarked that he would go out of this world as he had come into it, afraid and crying. There was no need to effect some artificial posture; Morita considered himself "nothing special." And in that very consideration he was extraordinary.

Mrs. Peiser's Practice

Even without formal individual study, some people have the capacity for firm understanding of constructive living. Here are some excerpts from letters written by Mrs. Jill Peiser, of Huntington, New York. You can see from this woman's writing that there are limits to limitations.

April 1

Although I've had no formal therapist with constructive living except from your books, I followed so many of your suggestions, difficult as they were for me. When you mentioned about writing thank you notes to people I wrote them, and I realized this week how ironic it is that I never wrote to you. So this is a small token of my appreciation.

I've cleaned the garbage in my neighborhood; I've done things when I felt lazy or scared (mostly scared), and I have been volunteering in a nursing home.

I am a thirty-seven-year-old woman with rheumatoid arthritis and many physical limitations. The last few years I suffered so much I went to some "conventional" Western therapy (before reading your ideas), which provided me with insight and understanding of my feelings but still left me nowhere as far as doing something with all of these insights. The bottom line is, I think, it is great to have these insights, but unless you are going to act upon them (or in spite of them) you still remain in your rut.

I have slowly begun to "grow up." Your teachings helped numerous friends and relatives with whom I have shared this knowledge. I got to the point in my life that I knew I had to make a decision—to sink or swim. I'm just getting my feet wet again, but I am determined to keep on going.

I keep referring to your books when needed and find help at each reading. In fact, I've been using your techniques when I visit the ill at the nursing home. When they tell me of their pain and their misery, I listen and acknowledge it politely, then ask them about the pictures of their grandchildren or compliment the women on the antique rings they are wearing. I see how just this shift in conversation helps them become less self-focused. It becomes a help to them as well as reinforcement for me. I want to keep coming back and doing more (when my physical condition permits) to get my mind off my own problems. It is all very hard, but I know I have no choice if I want a more fulfilling life.

I have a ten-year-old daughter with whom I can share some of the constructive-living fairy tales, but I wonder if you have ever thought of publishing an illustrated book for children. Why wait for them to grow up and become "messed up" before they can benefit from these teachings . . .

April 22
What a thrill it was for me to receive your kind letter with so much information concerning constructive living . . .

You asked if I would mind your using my letter or parts of it in print (with or without my name, as I wish). I was pleased to do so, but initially of course I don't want my name mentioned because I forgot the details of the letter. What if there was something personal in it? My mind went on and on. Then

I smiled to myself and decided in true Moritist spirit that I could feel embarrassed and tell you to certainly use my name. So whatever you believe would help other students please use, and please use my name if you wish. And if there is anything in this letter you'd like to print, I'd be honored.

I was especially struck by the last sentence in your letter: "Do what needs to be done." It really hit home to read it personally addressed to me even though I've read it so many times in your books. It came at a good time because, as you know, I have rheumatoid arthritis and much of my dilemmas come from conflicts concerning action and nonaction according to my physical condition. The day after receiving your letter I felt ill and frustrated because I wanted to go out and do things. I kept wrestling with whether it was worth doing things and possibly feeling much worse (which usually happens when I push myself) or doing "nothing" and staying mostly in bed. In a flash, your sentence came to mind. I realized that even resting is "doing what needs to be done," annoying as it may be. I'm always trying to be perfect, and I have trouble with my limitations. Your constructive-living maxim didn't take away all the frustration (that is fine) yet I still knew I was acting constructively by choosing to rest. In a sense, I felt less helpless. It is hard for me, because when I have to lie around so much I dwell on my problems. But I am learning. Thank you.

The other day when I felt sad I went to a nearby woods and cleaned up the garbage again. I actually laughed to see all the stares. A neighbor stopped by in her car to chat. When I got home, I noticed she was so inspired she was cleaning up her yard! So, you see, if we implement the teachings in our world, it's bound to have an effect on others. I also noticed that my cleaning was not some sort of ego trip for me. I didn't clean up for recognition or even so much to make my neighborhood look better. I did it because I knew it needed to be cleaned. Probably no one else would do it. It's interesting; if I feel good about do-

DAVID K. REYNOLDS

ing something like that for the world, that's a plus. But it's not essential and not the reason why I'm doing it.

One other story: Our fourteen-year-old dog ran away several days ago. A delivery person left the door open and the dog wandered out. The dog is pretty senile and hasn't run away for a long time, so we thought that was the end of him. My daughter, Annie, sat around crying. I told her she could feel sad and still do something that might help the situation. She got up and put our name and address on a picture of the dog and gave it to the postman—a good idea. She and her friends had a search party and were planning on a sign campaign for the surrounding area, still feeling miserable. I called the dog shelter again. Some Good Samaritan had found him and brought him in! Later that day, Annie and I talked about the lessons we learned from that experience. Thank you again!

Oh yes. I decided to thank the delivery person for all his help during the year and not focus on the one time he made a mistake (as hard as it is for me to do).

My Naikan Reflections at 35,000 feet

As you may know, I fear to fly. And yet I've been flying for more than thirty years. Within the past seven months I've flown to China, New York, Seattle, Japan, Australia, New Zealand, Miami, Washington, D.C., Hawaii, and back to Los Angeles again and again. In that short period I flew on more than a half dozen airlines and types of aircraft. Flew scared. But there were people who needed to hear words about constructive living and people who needed to see someone who, frightened, did what he needed to do anyway. So I flew, am flying at this very moment in a DC-10 over the Midwest headed for home.

Fears need not stop us from doing what is important for us to do—that message I have taught and lived for the past thirty years. Now, when even mild turbulence rattles us my hands perspire and my stomach tightens. My mind knows intellectually that all is well. I look around and see cabin crew going about their routine duties, standing and walking in the aisles. Fear isn't rational. It cannot be turned off by reasoning. Fear just comes as it will, not as I will it.

Now I'm reflecting on the efforts of others who are contributing to my flight. I'm held aloft here not only by those powerful

DC-10 engines, but by the labor of people—many of whom I've never met. Let's begin with the ground crew that serviced and fueled this plane, the designers and testers of the aircraft, and the test pilot(s) who risked their lives to see that the plane was airworthy. My travel agent went to the trouble to book this flight so that I would have a nonstop trip to Los Angeles. At Dulles airport a pleasant lady checked me in and passed along my baggage to handlers who packed it safely aboard for me. Another kind lady answered my nervous phone call this morning to reconfirm the reservation and departure time. She ended our phone exchange with the kind wish that I "have a pleasant trip."

There are a pilot and first officer on the flight deck. Standing invisibly behind them are their instructors and others who designed and built flight-instruction manuals and navigation equipment. Safety engineers built backup systems to improve my chances of arriving home safely.

The cabin crew serves my meals and otherwise distracts me from my anxiety with a film and magazines. They remind me of safety precautions and contingencies in case some problem should occur. So many people have considered my safety and have developed ways to preserve it!

Ground controllers pass my plane along from point to point so that we don't collide with other planes. They guide us to secure takeoffs and landings. How alert they remain for my safety!

You may say that all these people have been properly and amply paid for their services. I won't deny that they receive salaries in small part derived from the tickets I have purchased. But the fact remains that their efforts, their long hours and perspiration and careful thought and expertise permit me this rapid form of travel. And the money I used for the tickets, of course, wasn't mine. It was given to me by other people who kindly read my books and invited me to speak to them and agreed to publish my books. These people, too, hold me aloft in this reclining seat. As do the teachers who instructed me in the work I do, those who painstakingly taught me the Japanese language, and the parents who gave me this body and nurtured it during infancy and childhood. Thanks to those people, I could make a living and thus buy the ticket that allows me to fly today.

Perhaps some of those airline employees are thinking that they are only doing a routine job; perhaps some are doing only the minimum to get their paycheck; perhaps only a few, sometimes, consider me (or the passenger who I represent) as they go about their work. Nonetheless, the efforts of all these people keep me aloft. The result of their work keeps me flying even when their attitudes are less than ideal.

But then, my attitude is not always self-denying in service to those who count on me, either. How could I ask qualities of these tens of thousands of others that I don't exhibit myself? And yet I do ask such qualities from them. Self-centered creature that I am, I denounce the self-centeredness of others.

How can I complain when the flight doesn't proceed with absolute smoothness for my convenience? When I think of the tens of thousands of people who linked hands to reach from ground level to 35,000 feet in order to keep me flying, how can I feel anything but wonder and gratitude? Yet, again, I do. I feel fear, too, and a fervent wish to arrive soon and unhurt.

Foolish and self-centered though I am, my debt to my benefactors cannot be denied, mustn't be ignored. Thank you for this flight and the ones last Thursday and the one last week and the one before that and . . .

DAVID K. REYNOLDS

Casual Considerations

WHAT I DO

My eccentric habits of eating jelly in chili and chocolate almost any time help keep people from confusing themselves about who is their teacher. Their teacher is reality.

The other day I was asked to repeat a series of points I had made a week or so earlier at a lecture in another city. I couldn't remember what I had said then. I have difficulty remembering what I have written in my books, though I know well the principles on which the stories and essays are based. You see, I'm a car and not a garage.

Perhaps you think I have some special knowledge that I husband and mete out little by little. More often, however, the material appears as I go along.

A FEW GOOD MEN AND WOMEN

Like the marines, I'm looking for a few good men (and women, of course). Part of my work is undercover, in a way. One of my dreams is to intrigue a few people high up in the power hierarchy of our country. Perhaps they will be individuals who have it all and have become bored or they may have come to realize the emptiness of where they stand. I am looking for people in power who will risk what they have for constructive living, just because it is right and because it is realistic.

My goals are various. I'm not here to defend constructive living. That would be unnecessary. Reality does that. What I want to show you is the assumptions underlying your criticisms when they exist. I want you to see the source of your critique.

ABOUT WRITING

Writing is like making taffy. I fold the ideas over and over until they become firm and, hopefully, tasty.

Haiku are poetic examples of experiential operationalism. They don't describe feelings. Rather, they give directions or reminders of observations and behaviors that lead to specific feelings. Words are only analogies of experience; they aren't the experiences themselves.

The two main messages of my work are:
1) To social scientists: Admit experiential knowledge into your sphere of study/research techniques.
2) To all humans: Know your purpose, accept your feelings, do what needs doing, be reality-oriented.

It is sufficient for me simply to state these communications clearly and to publish them broadly. It is for others, then, to do what needs doing.

Two more book manuscripts were sent off to publishers this year. If everything is published, I'll have twenty different books published in Japan and the U.S. To think of writing so many books at once would be intimidating and impossible; but they were written one by one. Little by little, word by word, page by page, we write the stories of our lives without knowing the endings. Fortunately, we don't have to do everything at once.

Once I thought that ideas were gold. I treasured all the scattered notes written as thoughts popped up. Now I see that ideas

DAVID K. REYNOLDS

are like kids with potential. Potential isn't worth anything until it is properly developed through education, self-discipline, and hard work.

Ideas, too, lack worth until they are molded into usable form. The steps from inspiration through publication are much like those from latency through mastery.

When we write about writing or when Garry Shandling invites the studio audience to be a part of the show, we invite the consumers to be participants of the producers' in-group. How does that affect art? The performers? The audience?

I need whole days alone to write because when people are around, I'm drawn into standard exchanges, ordinary interaction, typical talk. Some people seem to be able to create and sustain novelty in the midst of socializing; I am a mirror.

The time alone allows my thoughts to settle and to travel. Isolation prompts a sort of meditation. I stand here before the keyboard focusing, focusing, attending, attending.

Most reporters write children's stories that masquerade as adult stories. I write adult stories that masquerade as children's stories.

Taking my words out of context is like trying to describe what kind of person I am while ignoring the situation I'm in.

SIMPLIFICATION

I like to put things in order, to simplify, to discover simplifying underlying principles. Even folding bedclothes, putting away dishes in their proper places, updating a database of addresses is pleasurable now and then.

The garden, too, simplifies my life. Only weeds, plants, and me. While I work in the garden, my feelings and thoughts run the gamut of "This is fun," "Why do I have to do this work (I don't),"
"How fascinating!" "How boring!" "Why don't others work harder on this garden?" "How can other people bear to work so hard over such a long time on this garden?" and on and on. All the while a track of essentially weed-free earth grows behind me.

Sometimes my students learn lessons from me that I didn't intend to teach them. Because they expect to be taught both directly and indirectly, they read special meaning into some of my words and deeds. It is that very lesson about being ready to learn that I want them to master. In constructive living our teacher is reality. I am merely another part of that reality for my students. When they grasp this key element of constructive living, they will be primed to learn a variety of lessons from all sorts of people—friends, salespeople, aged relatives, small children, street people.

In constructive living we never leave the student mode. Some lifeways encourage students to graduate into new roles of leadership with no further need for learning. Yet all of us need to remain students of reality.

PART III

THE TRAINING OF THE MIND

In this section we look at some of the practical assignments that are characteristic of constructive living. Koans are puzzles with solutions that help lead to deeper insights into constructive-living principles. Exercises are assignments with well-suited results for those who practice constructive living. Maxims help explain constructive-living principles in condensed form. And diaries are often assigned to seat the constructive-living perspective firmly in daily life.

Koans

"Koans are very difficult."
"So is life."
"But koans are more difficult than life."
"Do you think so?"

TURNING OFF A FAUCET

Three people turn off a dripping faucet: an ecologist, a Moritist, and a Naikanist. Each has a particular goal or purpose in turning off the faucet. If asked, each will offer a different reason for his or her behavior. What are the three reasons for turning off the dripping faucet?

WALKING

Walking, walking.
Slow uphill; fast downhill.
Walking, walking.

Breathing, breathing.
Fast uphill; slow downhill.
Breathing, breathing.

Notice walking and breathing continues.
Notice breathing and walking continues.
Walking while breathing.
Breathing while walking.
Nothing special.

WATERFALL

Waterfalling
Waterfell
Waterfalling

Exercise

This is the section you must master in order to understand constructive living. The other material is decorative, hopefully enticing, trim for the house in which you can live. My constructive-living colleagues have suggested some of the exercises. Their contributions and names are listed below.

"I loved your books!"

"Thank you. What exercises have you done?"

"Well, I haven't actually . . ."

"Then you have no idea what my books are really about."

COMMON SENSE

If you slam a door you must return to it, open it, and close it properly, and apologize to it for your insensitivity. If you leave a faucet dripping, you must shut it properly and apologize to it. If you leave a light or appliance on unnecessarily or break a pencil lead or drop a coin or kick up the corner of a rug or otherwise behave thoughtlessly, particularly if you are in haste or angry or otherwise upset at the time, you must correct the behavior and apologize to the offended object.

TELEVISION TAGS

Television programs provide a fine resource for sampling understandable American English speech and common American values. This exercise involves watching television in order to
distinguish the speech habits and values that underlie outmoded
ways of thinking about feelings. Drama shows (including soap op-
eras) display these themes most clearly, but news programs and
talk shows and documentaries exhibit these themes also.

* Notice misuse of the word *feel* to mean *think, believe, expect,
  hope, imagine,* and the like. How does this confusion (of the
  F word, as it is sometimes called in constructive living) cause
  difficulties for the characters in the television show?
* Notice the emphasis on the theme of feelings. What evidence is
  provided that feelings are more important than anything else?
  How does this emphasis on a directly uncontrollable aspect of
  human existence cause unnecessary problems for the characters
  in the television show?
* Notice the assumption that feelings must be expressed or they
  will fester and/or explode. Attention is rarely given to the third
  alternative of accepting feelings, for example. How does the pre-
  sumption that feelings must be expressed complicate the lives
  of the characters? What alternatives can you recommend to the
  characters on the basis of your understanding of constructive
  living?

TEST A FEELING IMPULSE

Find out the importance of an impulse to act. Don't act on it. Turn
your attention and behavior to some other activity. See if the impulse keeps emerging again and again. The frequency and strength
of the impulse tells you how important it is to you now. When an
impulse to do something keeps popping up in spite of your attention to other activities, it is worth careful consideration.

DAVID K. REYNOLDS

You may choose to act on the impulse or not after considering it carefully. That depends on whether acting on it helps you achieve some important goals in your life, like repaying someone you owe a favor, helping someone in need, avoiding the risk of causing trouble for someone else, and so forth.

INSIGHT

A form of this exercise has been suggested before, but it is worth repeating. As much as safety permits, do your morning routine with your eyes closed. Get dressed, brush your teeth, comb your hair with periods of closed eyes. Notice the sensory input from your other senses. Notice how the input from sight has dominated some activities. Give attention to the attention necessary to carry out these not-so-simple routine tasks.

HINTS FOR NAIKAN EXERCISES

Draw a map of the house in which you lived during the period assigned for Naikan reflection. Bring old photos of your family, a school annual, report cards, and other memorabilia. Only a limited number of memory aids should be used; too many objects allow distraction from Naikan.

SPEECHLESSNESS

We use two levels of silence in our assignments to students. One level is complete silence. Even then, however, the student may write notes as often as necessary. In practice, however, the student ordinarily uses writing very little. It is much more time-consuming and effortful to write than to speak.

The second level of silence is limited speech. The student may speak but must have a clear purpose before speaking. The words used must be succinct and carefully chosen.

Assignments of silence help the students see the value and limits of speech. These assignments also help the students discover the difference between feelings (such as the desire or impulse to verbalize) and behaviors (talking itself). They get practice in accepting the uncontrollable (the feelings) while maintaining control over behavior (speaking).

COUPLES EXERCISE

For quarreling couples, constructive-living instructors often assign a joint task, preferably one involving joint action in some volunteer program. Working alongside another person with a common goal offers the opportunity to develop closeness.

MORE EXERCISES

Meals with no self-serving. Try some meals with family or friends in which those gathered at the table are not permitted to serve themselves and cannot ask for what they want. You must watch the eyes of others, offer them and serve them various dishes. They may refuse an offer, but they may not ask for some alternative. They must wait until a desired dish is offered and accept it.

Add to the daily exercise of ten thank yous and ten I'm sorrys the task of saying each differently, using a variety of words and phrases.

Ration sentences to those who talk a lot. Those who try this exercise should begin with a ration of fifteen sentences per day.

Letting others go first—in taking food, in speech, in selecting assignments, in going through a door—put their convenience first.

Total up the number of meals prepared for you by your mother, the number of sheets she folded, the pairs of pants and shirts hung on a washline and the dishes she washed for you. Exact numbers, of course, are impossible to determine, but the effort of calculating as close as possible is useful.

Unobtrusively trace the movements and habits of other people in your life; get a fix on their movements, preferences, habits. See

DAVID K. REYNOLDS

what you can discover about their lives that you didn't already know.

Leave no trace. Pick up coffee cups, hair in bathroom, any signs that you have been somewhere other than your room.

Consider the specific contributions of others in allowing you to be at this particular place at this particular time. For example, the customers who bought the product that allowed the company to finance your business trip, the taxi driver who drove you to the hotel, the clerk who checked you in at the front desk, and so forth.

Suggested by Patricia Ryan Madson: Invite someone you would like to know better to come along with you while you do something ordinary: shopping, cooking, walking the dog, and the like. Do not be attached to whether the person accepts your invitation; he or she deserves to be invited.

Suggested by Michael Whitely: While in flight, write a letter to the airline company about praiseworthy actions performed by the crew. Be specific about the service; include names. Address and stamp the letter before landing.

Suggested by Ron Green: Make a gift for your spouse requiring some new skill or knowledge on your part.

Suggested by Yen Lu Wong: In this Siamese-twin exercise, husband and wife tie themselves side by side at the waist using a long, wide sash. It should be tight enough so that they must move as a single unit during the three-hour period of the exercise. During the three hours they may not speak or write but they may gesture and mime. Cooperating together, the spouse on the right may use only the right hand; the spouse on the left may use only the left hand.

The best time for the exercise is in the morning. The couple must discover how to get out of bed, brush their teeth, get dressed, make breakfast and eat it, wash dishes, and so forth. Having someone videotape the exercise will provide laughs and reflection later.

Suggested by Stan Tatkin: Write original bedtime stories for your children or grandchildren incorporating elements of wisdom you wish to pass on to them. Read the stories to them.

Maxims

Maxims are pithy ways of citing and recalling constructive-living principles. Again, contributions of my constructive-living colleagues are included below.

"I tape up a new maxim on my bathroom mirror every week."
 "Why?"
 "So I can memorize them."
 "Why memorize them?"
 "Just seems like a good thing to do."
 "And then?"
 "Then?"

Here are some recent constructive-living maxims. Most of them were created by constructive-living instructors during their training at the ten-day certification courses around the United States. I have included a short explanation for some of them.

When you fall, thank the ground for catching you.—Crilly Butler
 Don't do what needs to be not done.—Crilly Butler
 Do, don't stew.—Larry Andrews

It's been real.—Kate Bean (a constructive-living greeting)

When life throws you a curve . . . SWING!—Bob Brown

Reality will never tell you a lie, but I won't ask you to believe that.—Mary Ann Thomas

Food won't make you fat.—Mary Ann Thomas

The present is received whatever the wrapping paper.—Diana Peterson

Poison ivy and snakes illuminate the woods.—David Pollock (They invite us to pay attention during our walks through the woods.)

For a healing perception of reality the attitude is gratitude.—Gene Hoffman

Self-help books don't work.—Nicholas Callie, Jr. (People work.)

The more I look within, the more I find I'm without.—Joan Fischer

Constructive-living people do it on purpose.—David Hudson and Rami Shapiro

Put off procrastination.—Shana Alexander

Blossoms have no names.—(the author) (We give names to groups of flowers but not to individual blossoms. Perhaps they deserve names, too. That's Andy; there's Margaret. Are their lives too short for naming?)

Join reality and see the world; join reality and be the world.—(the author) (Constructive living bids us to live realistically, to pay attention to what reality brings. In time we learn that we not only live *in* reality, we actually live reality.)

Mindburgers or life meals.—(the author) (Many people seem to want their reality served ground, juicy, soft, and wrapped in small paper wrappings while served on disposable plastic trays. A few others seem to want a variety of courses in their lives, requiring effort both in preparation and in cleanup.)

Act is fact.—Ron Green

Wherever you go there you are; wherever you are someone helped you get there.—Ron Green

Even a rock lies on something.—Ron Green

Give yourself away; you weren't yours in the first place.—Ron Green

The following maxims were found mysteriously embedded in fortune cookies during certification training around the United States in 1989:

The ocean smooths the edges from rocks provided they stay in the ocean.

She sometimes calls for rescue from the lifeguard crew as she walks along the shore. Furthermore, she swims quite well (sometimes).

No journeys, only this step now. (A journey of a thousand miles notwithstanding.)

You are growing beyond one kind of Zen.

You show flashes of warm lightning in a quiet, cold storm.

No matter how high the leap, dance with feet firmly on the ground.

With eyes on the distant mountain, watch the winding path underfoot.

Prison break! You saw the outside over the wall; keep working on your tunnel to freedom.

Purposeful action gets the job done faster than humility.

Throw away old ways of thinking and speaking.

Simplify your life beyond cleverness—be a pearl not a diamond.

You are a fur-covered diamond, hiding brilliance and sharp edges.

Tired of wearing old clothes? Why keep wearing them?

You are a safe teddy bear with potential for becoming a zookeeper.

The gleam of insight and conning illuminates the need for unlearning.

Your self is shrinking as your world is growing.

DAVID K. REYNOLDS

Constructive-Living Journals

INTRODUCTION

Constructive-living diaries are written on pages divided vertically into columns for time, feelings (and other mental processes), and behaviors. The students write what they were thinking and feeling at a particular time in one column and what they were doing at that same time in another column. Behavior or doing or action is anything external, anything that could be caught by a video camera. Any internal, mental change is written in the other column. The diaries give students practice apportioning their everyday lives into (uncontrollable) feelings and (controllable) behaviors. Two representative diaries are offered below.

DIARY OF A YOUNG MAN

I have pulled together four excerpts from the diary of a young man who suffered from an anxiety reaction or panic disorder. He would worry that he was having a heart attack, call the paramedics, go to emergency clinics. Invariably, he would be told that there was nothing wrong with his heart. Relieved, he would return home only to have another attack within days or weeks.

The diary entries are from the thoughts and feelings column of the fourth, fifth, sixth, and seventh weeks of constructive-living instruction. My comments were written on the diary; they are included here in brackets. Notice the ups and downs of the suffering, the twisting and squirming of the mind. There is no steady climb out of harmful habits. Temporary setbacks and unexpected challenges are common.

1. "Feeling a bit concerned about pain in my chest but am accepting as anxiety or nothing serious. Funny, six months ago I would have compounded it by believing it to be a heart attack and concentrating on it. At least now I can deal with it reasonably. [Fine! That's the best anyone can do.] Intent upon doing and let the chips fall. I can't control where they may fall or, more accurately, where they will fall. I can only do my part; that's all I am responsible for and can always do what my part is."

2. "Getting neurotic about thinking that my pulse is now too slow! [The struggle continues, but you are winning. You will soon be in control of you.] That's a twist after palpitations were driving me crazy. I could just imagine going to my doctors (who think I am a hypochondriac to begin with) with that complaint. I am wondering, could Morita therapy allow one to acknowledge a symptom that indeed needs attending to, then go about business? Sometimes anxiety symptoms and symptoms of more serious illnesses seem to be the same." [Have regular medical checkups.]

3. "Feeling pretty bad. That's a wrong word. Let's say I was more or less not as good as I was. I thought again I was having a heart attack because of chest pains. But I really see it's being anxiety more so than before. It's almost predictable, that is, the symptoms and my reactions. You'd think I'd learn. But I think I am. You were right; my progress has fluctuated. But I know what is happening and how to deal with it, and that's a big step." [Yes, it is. Furthermore, the more you involve yourself in constructive action, the less attention you will invest in annoying symptoms.]

DAVID K. REYNOLDS

4. "Feeling okay. Just a little anxiety but am developing ways to cope, and they appear to be becoming a part of my attitude. The change is positive. It definitely helps to alleviate the anxiety. [Eventually, you won't care so much whether you feel anxious or not. You will just continue about your business or play or listening or reading or whatever. "Hello, Anxiety. You again? Come on along, but I'm busy now."] The more I learn that the anxiety is harmless and that I've overreacted to a reaction, it appears almost laughable. However, it's still 'not there' totally. That is, I don't have it under control, but am getting a good look at my 'friend' and getting to know him for what he really is."

The changing attitude toward anxiety can be seen in the progression of the diary entries. The first entry seems full of confidence, but it is based primarily on intellectual understanding. He has the theory but has yet to test it and build experiential understanding. In the second entry a new variation of his anxiety attack has occurred. It is clear that he is still excessively focused on what is happening with his heart. Whether anxiety is present or not, his attention needs to be directed more on external reality and doing what needs doing. His question about the possibility of missing genuine symptoms receives a realistic response—have regular checkups. The beginning student's mind is filled with what-if's. The teacher's mind is filled with realistic action.

The third entry is still somewhat feeling-centered. But the student seems to be recognizing old habits of thinking and action as they appear, not always in retrospect. The fourth journal entry shows a suitable recognition of the difficulty of this lifeway. There is still some feeling-centeredness, but there is also humor and some beginning acceptance of the anxiety. Use of the word *friend* in referring to the anxiety would have been unthinkable earlier on in the instruction. We aim not only for tolerance but for a genuine acceptance of anxiety. In this case it springs from the natural desire to preserve life and health. It is a true friend.

As usual, when my student made friends with his symptoms, they stopped showing up. But such a friendly relationship isn't created merely by reading a book or believing that such an attitude makes sense. As you may know . . .

A WOMAN'S DIARY

TIME	FEELING	BEHAVIOR
8/4/87		
7:00 A.M.	Sleepy, want to go back to sleep. Had to go to the bathroom. Felt bad about the coming of the day and wondered about things to do today. Wondered if I should get hair cut. Desire to do it, but enough money?	Stayed in bed a bit, read, rested eyes. Got up, went to bathroom. Made something to drink. Straightened up, dishes, put away clothes.
7:30 A.M.	Felt pretty good and proud of myself for getting up and finally tuning in on TV exercises.	Turned on TV for yoga recommended by M.D. Watched instructor and tried to imitate.
7:45 A.M.	Felt a bit angry about being interrupted by phone.	Phone rang, talked to end of program.
8:00 A.M.	Feeling anxious about what was going on with book I'm reading.	Shut off TV and began to read book.
9:15 A.M.	Feeling somewhat sleepy again, also some accomplishment. Felt wonder at this assignment and felt guilty. [Feelings come and	Put book down. Lying on bed and fell asleep. [Stay out of bed except for night sleeping.]

TIME	FEELING	BEHAVIOR

go, build your life on behavior.]

8/6/87

7:30 A.M.	Feeling bad; terrible head-ache. Feel good that I'm forcing myself to do exer-cises in spite of headache.	Turned on TV set. Did yoga exercises. [Forcing yourself or not, the reality is that you did the exercises.]
8:00 A.M.	Still feeling headache. Felt somewhat good about making phone call.	Turned off TV. Made phone call.
8:35 A.M.	Still in same frame of mind. Felt somewhat good about making phone call but felt worried that someone stole food stamps, won't get them this month in time.	Made another important and long overdue phone call. [Satisfaction is often a natural result of doing what needs doing.]
8:45 A.M.	Still worried and wondered what to do about stamps. Will they arrive today? Decided to worry later if they haven't arrived. Felt guilty about not doing assignment daily as planned. [If you worry, worry, but keep on doing constructive activities. When you feel guilty feel it fully. The important thing is that you did the diary assignment today.]	Looked at list of things to do today. Decided to do assign-ment. [*Did assignment.*]

8/9/87

7:30 A.M.

Feeling depressed, sleepy. Frustrated about the day and things I *had* planned to do. [Plans must be modified to fit what reality brings.] On the verge of tears. Want to go back to sleep and forget it for a while. [When you wake up, get up.] I have no transportation, someone probably have ["has," pay attention when writing, too.] stolen my stamps. I won't be able to go shopping today.

Stayed in bed. Then turned on TV. Switched channel to yoga. Watched, then tried [?] to participate. Then laid on bed till program was over and then some (a bit of Mr. Rogers!). Turned off set.

[Again, wake up; get up.]

8:00 A.M.

Feeling a bit better and glad I forced myself into doing exercises. [Good feelings, bad feelings, all feelings come and go.] Still feeling depressed and lethargic. Wanting to cry.

Lying on bed, eyes closed, then open. Answer phone, eyes closed. [Do you see any connection between lying in bed and lethargy?]

8:15 A.M.

Feeling a little better and more in control of myself. [No need to feel in control; just do what needs doing.] Feeling that I must try to force myself to at least try to get some errands done. [No need to try or force yourself; just do errands.]

Completed a phone call.

DAVID K. REYNOLDS

| 8:30 A.M. | Feeling the same, but trying to change behavior. [Just change what you do. No need to fix feelings or intent.] | Got up, made bed, straightened things. Got robe and walked to shower. [Good!] |

8/10/87

7:00 A.M.	Sleepy, a strange feeling inside. Confused and very scared and distracted. [Watch feelings change through the day. Create a new attitude.]	Got out of bed, went to bathroom, straightened things up, cried.
7:30 A.M.	Same feelings, but now a little calmer.	Made phone call, talked.
8:00 A.M.	Still confused, strange inside. A bit scared but calmer. [Sometimes calmer, sometimes not. Keep behavior steady.]	Ended phone call. Made bed.
8:15 A.M.	Same feelings as above.	Walked to bathroom and took a shower.
8:45 A.M.	Feeling better. Still confused but a lot calmer and more in contact. [You use psychological terms in your own way. Let's talk about their meaning.]	Walked from shower. Treated sore on dog's paw. Dressed. Made up and dried hair. Listened to TV.
9:10 A.M.	Feeling gray, subdued perhaps. Not really happy or feeling much of anything but just going through the	Dressed and took dog out. [While not feeling much of anything you took care of your dog's needs. Fine!]

motions. [Most people most of the time aren't feeling happy or anything else. Their attention is on what they are doing.]

| 9:20 A.M. | Same as above. Also thought of upcoming day. How am I going to get to my destination? What about money? etc. [Reality brings real problems that require your attention and planning. Ruminating about feelings doesn't get those problems solved.] | Came back from short walk. Gave biscuits to dog, food to goldfish. Watered plant, turned off TV. [When not watching television, keep it off.] Counted change for bus and left for bus stop. |

What can we say about this journal? real financial and other life problems face this woman. They must not be ignored in her quest for psychological health. Fortunately, the very methods that will bring her a more satisfying psychological state will also involve her actively in changing her material and social life. The extreme focus on feelings pulls her away from doing what needs to be done to effect changes in her material life. Part of her wants to lie in bed and hide from her circumstances in drowsiness. As her diary suggests, some results of hiding out from reality may be headaches, guilt, confusion, and other unpleasant feelings. Meanwhile, the dog needs to be fed and walked.

Ms. E knows that her reality problems won't go away as she lies in bed. She recognizes the feelings of satisfaction that emerge as she works to change her life situation. But she continues to insert intermediate steps—try to, force myself to, straighten out my confusion, restore my mind, improve my attitude, and so forth.

DAVID K. REYNOLDS

P A R T   I V

CONSTRUCTIVE-LIVING TALES

Stories are part of reality. Like all of reality, they offer us lessons worth learning. And the lessons aren't the same for all of us. What is each story below trying to say specifically to you?

The tales presented near the end of this section were written by Gregg Krech, Mary Ann Thomas, and Robert Addleton, certified constructive-living instructors. I am grateful to have their permission to publish these stories.

Finally, I included some themes from children's stories and nursery rhymes along with hints about how to give them constructive-living interpretations.

Thirsty, Swimming in the Lake

    In a country doctor's office on a Tuesday morning, I overheard the following conversation. It was a metered exchange, with long pauses near the end.

    "Nobody ever really cared about me."

    "Nice looking clothes you're wearing, Ed. Pick them out yourself?"

    "No, my wife did that. But as I was saying, Doc—"

    "How long did you go to school?"

    "I wanted to drop out, but my mother made me—"

    "What did you have for breakfast this morning, Ed?"

    "Just coffee. And I fixed it myself. Margie hates getting up in the morning. If she loved me more than that damn down quilt—"

    "You slept at home last night?"

    "Of course. Why—"

    "I'm glad you made it safely to the office this morning, Ed."

    "Huh?"

    "Thirsty, swimming in the lake."

    "What?"

    "I said, 'Thirsty, swimming in the lake.'"

    "Doc, are you trying to tell me I should be grateful for what I've got?"

"Not at all, Ed. But it's important to notice the lake."

"All right, all right. But I feel so insecure. You know, Doc, that farming is such a gamble. We've got debts to worry about. And they say they're ruining the atmosphere and a drought is gonna hit us."

"We can't walk on water, Ed. Have to swim."

"Hmmm. Reckon you're right. Don't feel like swimming much sometimes."

"Yep, me either."

"Sometimes dog-paddling is the best I can do to keep from drowning."

"Yep, me too, Ed."

"Well, okay. I see what you mean. Thanks, Doc. Appreciate the time . . ."

"Glad you came by, Ed. Same lake, after all."

DAVID K. REYNOLDS

Rock Talk

Today, walking along the beach, I spotted a rock, slick and shiny. It attracted my attention, and I picked it up. But on closer inspection it turned out to be shiny because it was wet. As it dried, the rock became ordinary. It was just a rock. I was disappointed at first, and I almost threw it away. But the rock had been wonderfully smoothed by the sand and the waves. Although it was merely a plain rock ground smooth by the elements, it turned out to be worth keeping, even treasuring.

I found another rock as I walked the beach today. It, too, had been ground down and polished by reality. It had no sharp edges anymore. When I walk too fast I miss these small, smooth rocks that so fascinate me. They are my cousins, somehow, models of what I would like to become. But here I am now.

Good Ol' Days

In the twenty-second century, a new form of psychotherapy allowed patients to travel back in time and correct the mistakes of the past. Lani was thrilled. She knew in intimate detail the errors in her past, both her parents' and her own. She relished the opportunity to return to her childhood, adolescence, and young adulthood in order to repair her damaged, flawed history. Knowing what she knew now, it should be a snap.

She wondered at the enigmatic smile on her therapist's face as she latched the door of the time machine. And Lani felt somewhat perplexed by that final suggestion to "take it as it comes, expected or not." She knew exactly what she wanted to change and pretty much how she was going to change it.

The first scheduled stop was the evening her father forbade Lani to continue seeing Bud, the senior with a Harley Davidson road bike. Lani remembered that night as the beginning of her submitting to male dominance. She remembered her anger and resistance, but she had never dated Bud again. If she could have defied her father that night, what independence and courage she might have achieved in her life!

When she reemerged in time, Lani found herself seated in her young high-school body looking out with an adult's mind. She was dumbfounded for a moment. The room—yes, there had been those paisley drapes on the window, and Tim's Navaho blanket thrown over the back of the sofa. She hadn't thought of them for years. Her father was just beginning the lecture about Bud. But Dad looked so young! Had he really looked this way in the past? And he was talking with tears in his eyes! Lani hadn't remembered that. Her mind's eye held a memory of a giant old man hovering over a tiny girl and forcing his will on her. She could see the concern in his eyes as well as the determination to make his point strongly.

Furthermore, almost as a shadow in her mind, she could sense the thoughts and feelings of the high school Lani she had been. This high school Lani was somewhat fearful of her father, but she was also fearful of Bud. This younger Lani felt upset that her father was lecturing her like this, but she also felt some relief that she could slip out of the relationship with an unpredictable and some-times irresponsible Bud while blaming the breakup on her father's outmoded authoritarian ways. Lani hadn't remembered this aspect of the exchange with her father at all.

Lani's adult mind let the scene play out just as it had in the past. Until she could think through the consequences of changing these newly discovered variables, it would be better to leave well enough alone. Her past wasn't as simply constructed as she had thought. So *that* was what her therapist had meant.

As Lani skipped through the key events of her past (or so she had determined them from her adult perspective), she found those events more complicated than she had remembered. As she sam-pled the mind of Lani at sixteen and twenty and thirty, she could understand better the quandaries confronting her and the decisions she made at the time. That is not to say that Lani found nothing she might change in her past, but rather that the changes were fewer and less clear-cut. And Lani began to wonder whether she had, in fact, selected the key events of her past to examine at all.

When Lani returned to her twenty-second-century present, there was quite a change in her. That change was the result of a changed perspective and not the result of the targeted changes to her past.

Withdrawal by Computer

There came a time when some executives in major companies began to withdraw from human interaction. They spent their time closeted with their computers using elaborate spreadsheet software to make detailed graphs and charts.

Computers, you see, are simpler, more predictable, and more compliant than humans. Computers do what they are told, precisely and without grumbling. Unlike wives and husbands and children and lovers, computers are obedient. Literally obedient.

Lamentably, computers haven't the range and unpredictability of humans. They haven't the imagination and will of humans. They fail to present humans with the variety of challenges and obstacles accorded us by our fellows. Television comes closer, but still fails. Some executives preferred the fingerlike realities of television to the whole body of everyday reality. But they, too, became bored after a time.

Some of the closeted executives emerged from their work spaces to confront a diverse world again when they tired of the limitations of computers. But some remained shut off from the rest of the world by their semiconductor guardians. Their eyes grew somewhat rectangular, and their pupils darted back and forth in short jumps like cursors. They felt anxious unless their hands rested on a keyboard or a mouse. And they wondered if their dissatisfaction with life was basically a hardware or a software problem.

One day a hard disk failed and a computer executive found himself with a free morning. He hadn't been far from his desk in weeks, so he decided to take a walk in the park near his office building. In the park he saw an old man sitting on a large rock. Sometimes the old fellow tumbled off the rock and had to climb on it again. Sometimes he slapped the rock until his hand (and the rock?) hurt. Often, while slapping and kicking the rock, he lost his balance and fell off. But he never seemed satisfied walking around below the rock. He always found himself climbing on it again.

What a fellow! thought the executive. He turned around and headed back to see if the technician had arrived to fix the computer.

The computer fan was humming softly. Mysteriously, the screen scrolled the following message:

"The author of Hagakure, a Japanese classic about samurai life and ethics, didn't think much of what might be translated as 'technicians.' The problem with technicians, as he saw them, is that they aren't well rounded. From the constructive-living perspective, we might point out the rounding, the shaping and polishing of humans, comes from our interaction with reality. When we limit that interaction to a narrow sphere (defined, for example, as the space in front of a computer terminal), we shrink ourselves to fit that environment.

"There is something that prompts us to do our best when we are doing less than that in our current life. There is a voice that prompts us to change to more difficult work when we have mastered a task, when we are doing our best at work that is less than the work of which we are capable. You will hear that voice, for example, if you are capable of being a fine author but you are delivering newspapers very competently. Many don't know that latter voice because they are not yet doing the best they can at their current work."

Venus

Once upon an unreal, and magical time, a lovely young lady wished for an ageless, firm figure and an eternally calm mind. At last she was granted her wish by the gods.

You may find her in the rose garden alongside the other statues.

Sunrise

Imagine a country in which the populace spent long hours trying to make the sun rise and set. They worked hard at making objects fall in a downward direction. They strained to cause their hearts to beat and their breath to flow in and out and their temperatures to go up and down.

They didn't waste a lot of time treating each other kindly and respectfully. They believed such behavior should come naturally, without hypocrisy. They didn't set practical goals or work to achieve life purposes because they thought such activities artificial and primitive.

In this far land the people judged the human depth and value of others by the liveliness of their temperatures. Bedridden invalids were highly respected if their temperatures got high enough or low enough or especially if they spiked up and down. Professions were devoted to showing temperature spikes on television and in film. Other ways to attain distinction in this country were to accumulate colored paper or to mold face and body into a standard form created by paper merchants.

No citizens with any influence wished to speak out against the foolishness of the customs because they feared risking their privileges and inviting some retaliation. Those in power kept to their beds, aspiring for temperature spikes.

The only hope for the citizens of this strange land was that someday enough people would get tired of the lunacy, even get tired of the winning, and change priorities. But those who risked giving up what they already had would have to be considerably crazy, don't you think?

Singing Apples

They were called singing apples, though the sound they put forth was more like a whistle than a song. The new breed of apple announced its ripeness with a chorus that built and built until the apples released their hold on the branches and fell into the inverted canvas umbrellas stretched beneath the trees. Very convenient.

Those who worked in the orchards were used to the tumult, but visitors sometimes found the sounds eerie. The apples seemed almost joyous giving themselves away. They found their way into pies and ciders and tarts and salads and the like. Very commendable.

They were rather simple-minded in their behavior. And their form of expression was limited to a single channel. But their single-minded purpose was accomplished straightforwardly and without fuss for anyone. Very clever.

Some consumers ate the apples with no thought of the years of effort that went into breeding them, the toil of the packers and shippers and grocers, the sacrifice of the apples themselves. But some people, some of the time, noticed the largess involved. Very creditable.

Leer

Two scholars drove past a couple of seedy-looking males leering at a passing lady. The academics remarked about the pity that those disreputable-looking people must escape from their misery by focusing their attention on the unfortunate woman. Meanwhile, the scholars, too, were escaping from their misery by focusing their intellectual discussion on the seedy characters.

So the writer writes . . .

Changes

Once upon a time, an extraordinarily ordinary person named Lee suffered from cancer. Lee was not better than other people. Lee was not worse than other people. Lee was neither stronger nor weaker than others. The difference between Lee and most other people was that Lee had cancer.

Lee tried to figure out why. Why me? Why this disease? Why now? Difficult questions. And the answers Lee heard from others weren't very satisfying. Furthermore, the answers Lee conceived weren't any more satisfying. So Lee had to live every day without a clear understanding of why reality sent this disease this way at this time.

Sometimes Lee felt hopeful, sometimes hopeless. Sometimes Lee felt sicker, sometimes better. Sometimes Lee even forgot the cancer altogether. How could someone forget such a thing even for a moment, you may wonder. But I ask you, have you ever forgotten to taste a delicious meal when you got involved in an interesting conversation at dinner? Has your attention ever slipped away from the tired and sore muscles as you accepted your sports trophy? Did you have the experience of forgetting your trouble and expense when someone beamed a thank you for the gift you presented? We can't pay attention to everything at once, thankfully.

Lee was always changing. Lee's world was always changing. Lee's attention was always shifting, too. One trend I noticed in the Lee-with-cancer, however, was a tendency to serve other people more than before. Lee thought more about others' convenience than ever before. Pretty remarkable, I thought. Just at a time when you might expect Lee to focus on personal problems and private feelings, this person was spotlighting the needs of family and fellow patients and even the staff who provided medical and human services. I asked Lee about this tendency.

Again, the why of it all is unclear, how it got started. But Lee says that when involved with others' lives, when assisting them to deal with the hurdles of life, Lee's own misery seems distant, somehow. At least some of the time.

Lee keeps up the struggle with cancer. Wholeheartedly. But life is more than fighting cancer. You can't duel with this opponent all day every day. In the in-between times Lee gives Lee away to others. And, for a while, Lee becomes Greg and Cynthia and Andy and Rosamartha. Where is the worry about cancer then?

For Old Times' Sake

"We find the defendant guilty, Your Honor."

"Mr. Axelman, you have been found guilty by a jury of your peers. You are hereby sentenced to an injection of twenty years. The court physician will perform her duty. Court is adjourned."

The nineteen-year-old youth bared his arm and scarcely winced as the clear fluid was injected into his vein. The doctor placed the alcohol-soaked cotton ball against the small puncture wound and flexed the man's arm to hold it in place. Then she turned without a word and left the courtroom.

Within minutes the convicted felon was on the street, too. But his steps were noticeably slower than before. He felt older already but not wiser. He was already sizing up nearby pedestrians for their potential as victims. He would be needing cash soon.

The next arrest came within a week of the first injection. He hadn't been able to run as fast as in his youth. And the alcohol in his bloodstream interfered with his thinking more than it had in the past. A second offense, the sentence was twenty-five years. The needle looked exactly the same; he could discern no difference in the amount of fluid in the syringe.

The sentence was carried out swiftly, as before, but it took him much longer to get out of the courtroom and onto the street. His legs felt heavy and there was a dull ache below the ribs where he had been punched during the scuffle with the arresting officers last week. Funny, he hadn't noticed that ache before. He shuffled when he wasn't paying attention to walking properly. His shoulders were bent forward. He felt chilled. Within a day or two his hair would be gray.

Of course, sixty-four years of age isn't the end of one's life these days. Those who age naturally adapt. But those who receive the aging censure from society find the sudden changes shocking to mind and body.

The prisons are nearly empty; electric chairs are museum pieces. A few crimes are committed by people in their eighties or nineties, but they are easy to catch. We shelter and feed the "old-shots," but medicine makes no heroic efforts to save them from their natural deaths.

Very efficient. Very humane. All that research on physiological aging was useful, after all.

DAVID K. REYNOLDS

No Pain, No Pleasure

—by Gregg Krech

Glen learned that all four of his wisdom teeth had to be pulled. Upon hearing the dentist's words, Glen winced and broke out in a cold sweat. When he called his girlfriend in New Zealand, she offered to time her next visit to the U.S. to coincide with Glen's dental surgery. Glen was elated. Sue would be nearby to ease the pain.

On the day of the extraction the dentist told him, "Don't worry, your mouth will be so numb you won't feel a thing." And to Glen's surprise, the dentist was right. After the operation, Glen heard, "In a couple of hours the numbness will start to fade, and you'll feel some pain. If you take one of these pills, your mouth will be numb again for a few hours and you won't be able to feel a thing."

Glen returned home and discovered Sue waiting there. She greeted him with a big hug and a soft kiss on the lips. To Glen's dismay, he couldn't feel her kiss at all.

"I'm sorry," she said, noticing the lack of his usual response to her kiss. "Did I hurt you?"

"No," Glen replied with disappointment. "In fact I couldn't even feel your kiss."

Before long the anesthetic began to fade. What began as a subtle soreness turned into a throbbing pain.

"Oh, you poor thing." Sue consoled him with a kiss.

To Glen's surprise, he could actually feel her kiss. He recalled the first time they met in New Zealand, their happy days together there.

But the pain was so great that he took a pill. Within minutes his mouth was numb again. However, he was once more unable to enjoy Sue's kisses. What a dilemma! When his mouth was alive, he could delight in the demonstration of his girlfriend's affection. But such delight required him to bear the pain in his mouth. He could avoid the pain by putting his mouth to sleep, but to do so deprived him of the pleasure of Sue's kiss. Glen knew that the pain in his mouth would fade over time and he would no longer need the pills. But he also knew that Sue's visit would be brief. If he could only shut off the pain without shutting off the pleasure. But that resolution was impossible. Ultimately, he had to choose to accept both pain and pleasure or numb himself to both.

We must make similar choices again and again in our daily lives. Our behavior demonstrates/equals the choices we make.

Obstacle Along the Way

—by Gregg Krech

One sunny Sunday morning I set out along a new trail in the Blue Ridge Mountains. The trail ran along a rocky creek, winding through dense forests of pine, hemlock, and maple. Winds and storms had left numerous fallen trees and limbs to block the path. Sometimes it was necessary to detour around the obstacles.

After a few hours of effort I reached the summit. Magnificent views stretched before me. A cool breeze soared up the valley walls. As I sat and enjoyed the vista, my mind returned to the difficulties of getting around the fallen timber on my way up the path. I remembered distinctly an area of hurdles along the trail and a tree with a double trunk and difficult passage. How much easier it would have been if someone had cut away the fallen timber leaving only a pleasant, unobstructed path all the way to the top.

Then I remembered that some of the underbrush had been cut away to clear the path. Among all the detours there had been places where limbs and roots had been removed, leaving the trees standing alongside the trail. How interesting it was that I could clearly remember those trees that blocked my way, but only with the greatest of effort could I recall that obstacles had been removed.

As I descended the mountain, I noticed that there were quite a few of the cropped trees alongside the path. I decided to do some informal research. For a fifteen-minute period I counted the trees that were obstacles and those that had been cut to clear the path. The former were easy to count. If I didn't pay attention to them, I tripped and fell. The latter, however, required attention to notice because I had to scan the borders of the path for cut timber. At the end of the period I had counted forty-two trees that had to be overcome and forty-seven trees that had been cleared to make the path easier. The reality was that during my ascent there was more done to provide for a clear, unimpeded walk than was left to cause me difficulty. Yet it was the difficulty, the obstacles, that stood out in my memory.

This hike up the mountain resembles our lives. We notice the obstacles because we have to get around them without falling. And while we're figuring out how to get around them we don't pay much attention to those elements of reality that support our success and achievement. By paying attention to a wider vision of reality we can notice and appreciate those people and objects and energies in our lives that help to make the path a little easier.

DAVID K. REYNOLDS

Casino Reality

—by Gregg Krech

The sheer size of the room was overwhelming. In fact, Mr. Overton wasn't even sure if it was a room. He couldn't actually see any walls or windows. All he could see was an endless expanse, with people grouped around tables playing some sort of card game. There was bright light coming from above, but Mr. Overton couldn't see any light fixtures or ceiling. In front of him was a small table with a stack of gray booklets titled *Blackjack: Rules for Best Play*. He scanned the pages and recognized a set of guidelines for playing a game that seemed, at least on the surface, to be the casino game of blackjack. The booklet appeared to offer advice about the best play in any game situation. For example, on page 37 it read, "When the dealer has a picture card face up, the player should take another card if his total is 16 or less." Mr. Overton thought the book would be quite useful. He wandered over to the nearest table.

There were no empty seats, so he stood and watched. A group of people were gathered around the crescent-shaped table. Two cards were dealt to each player and to the dealer. The first card was always down and the second was faceup. Each player tried to get a point total as close as possible to 21. If the player went over 21, the game was lost. However, Mr. Overton could sense some difference from Las Vegas gaming. For one thing, what kind of casino would offer a book describing the most probable ways of winning the game?

To his amazement, there was no dealer behind the table. The cards seemed to be dealing themselves. They appeared from nowhere before each player with a corresponding hand for the non-existent dealer.

How strange, thought Mr. Overton. How could the game be played without a dealer? Who would keep an eye on shuffling and cheating? Nevertheless, the cards kept coming to each player at a steady pace, without pause, until the players gave a hand signal indicating that they would stick with their holdings. Mr. Overton strolled over to watch an attractive lady play her hand. She received a 6, bringing her total to 15. She seemed to be debating whether to take another card when a card appeared in front of her anyway. It was an 8. Her total was over 21. In an instant her cards and her wager disappeared into thin air. "Hey," she cried out. "I hadn't decided yet if I wanted another card." Her complaints went unnoticed by the other players as the game continued around the table. She turned to Mr. Overton. "I should have stuck at 15. I knew it. I could just kick myself for even considering another card." He was about to agree when he realized that her next hand had already been dealt. "Excuse me, I think it's your turn again." Before she could turn around to look at her cards, her turn to play had passed, leaving her with a hand that lost easily to the phantom dealer's hand of 19.

"See what you made me do," she scolded Mr. Overton. "It's your fault I lost that hand. If you hadn't distracted me, I would have won it." As she spoke, he noticed that she was about to lose another hand. He decided to slip away to another table.

As his eyes scanned the other nearby tables, he noticed an old man with bald head and gray beard who seemed to be smiling while concentrating on his cards. He moved over to watch that fellow play a few hands. The man won ten hands in a row. "What a streak of luck!" Mr. Overton congratulated him.

146

The old man glanced up. "There is no luck here," he remarked. "Luck is simply your explanation for my winning hands." He promptly won another hand.

"But you have been dealt winning hands eleven times in a row. Surely you must acknowledge that some luck is involved."

The old man looked him directly in the eye, then immediately turned his attention back to the game. "I get the cards I am dealt. I cannot control that. Then I play each hand the best I can. Sometimes I win and sometimes I lose, but I always play the best I can."

Mr. Overton noticed a worn copy of the gray manual lying on the table. He picked it up. "By following the guidelines in this book you are assured of winning?"

"Not necessarily," sighed the old man. "Watch."

He lost five of the next ten hands. On the next hand he had a total of 19, compared to the dealer's 18. He should have won, but his wager disappeared as though he had lost.

"I played as well as I could. Sometimes the best play loses anyway. In this game, when you lose you simply play the next hand. The important thing is to play well."

"But that last hand wasn't fair! You should have won!"

"No more questions." The old man kept his eyes on the cards. "Read the book, then come back."

So Mr. Overton found an empty chair away from the tables and began to read the book. Some of the guidelines were quite specific, but some were ambiguous and several were downright confusing. For example, one passage read: "In this situation the proper play is determined by the cards. Ask the cards what to do." Elsewhere it read: "When you find yourself in this difficult situation, you will know what to do." How could such guidelines be useful?

Back at the playing table, the old man continued to play each hand carefully. He played as though he were the only player in the casino and each hand was the first of his life. Once again Mr. Overton noticed him lose a wager on a hand that appeared to be won. "Isn't there someone you can complain to and get your rightful winnings?" he asked.

The old fellow chuckled. "That happens all the time. Some people get upset when that happens. Some spend hours running around the casino looking for someone to fix the problem. But it's no use. People expect to be rewarded for a winning hand, but the game doesn't always turn out that way. Sometimes even a winning hand loses. That's simply part of the game. All you can do is play the next hand and play it well."

"But that's not fair," complained Mr. Overton.

"No, it isn't," responded the old man as he continued playing.

Suddenly, a middle-aged man seated at the same table was dealt a faceless, blank card. The moment it hit the table, the man disappeared. Mr. Overton, startled, asked what happened.

"When a player is dealt a blank card, the game is over," the old man explained in a gentle voice, putting his hand briefly on Mr. Overton's shoulder.

"But what happened to him?"

"I don't know. I just know he's gone. Some players have come up with descriptions of what happens to someone when the game is over. All I know is that they're gone."

"Why don't people just leave the table to avoid that blank card?" Mr. Overton wanted to know. "Wouldn't it be safer just to walk away from the table and avoid the risk?"

"That's not possible." The cards kept coming. "There is no time out in this game. You can shift your attention, you can walk away from the table, you can just sit there. Whatever you do, the cards keep appearing at your place. The game goes on until it's over for you."

Mr. Overton found the prospect of playing with no time out disturbing. What an incredible game! It was played with blank cards, confusing guidelines, no visible dealer, winning hands that sometimes lose, and no time out.

"Do you enjoy playing this game?" he wondered.

"Sometimes I do," the player replied with a smile, "and other times I don't. But I keep playing. What else can I do? As long as I have the opportunity to play, I must play the best game possible."

148

When Mr. Overton glanced again at the gray manual, it appeared that some of the guidelines had changed. They seemed to have rewritten themselves. How could that be? He carried his book back to the table.

"I think there is something wrong with my book. The guidelines seem to have changed."

"Of course," explained the old man. "As you learn from the cards, the book adjusts itself. Neither the book nor I can teach you how to play. It is the playing that teaches you. The manual merely reflects what you already know."

"You mean if I continue to watch I will learn more about the game and my book will continue to rewrite itself?"

"You can learn by observing the game up to a point. But watching has its limits; by watching, you will never really understand the game."

"How, then? How can I truly understand the game?" Mr. Overton wanted to know.

"Just play." The old man motioned to an empty chair.

Mr. Overton understood. He smiled his thanks and sat down to play his first hand.

Worthless Complaints

—by Mary Ann Thomas

A young apprentice said to his master, "I will live the life of a self-made man. I am able to see that life can be good even though my father and mother were both worthless. My mother ran off long ago, and my father is the village drunkard."

"Ah," said the master. "A pity the two rascals were ever born."

The Wizard

—by Robert Addleton

Once there was a wizard who was reputed to be a great healer of neurotic suffering. People traveled from all corners of the kingdom for healing. He was quite busy, of course, and long waits were expected by those who sought him in hope of cure.

At the wizard's clinic, patients were shown to a waiting room. The wait was so long that they read books, wrote letters, knitted sweaters, and cleaned out their purses while waiting. The wizard's staff even invited the waiting patients to clean up the waiting room and office to pass the time while waiting. Brooms and mops and rags were available for that purpose.

Some of the patients noticed their neurotic complaints lessened or even went away while they were waiting to see the wizard. Others decided that their psychological aches and pains were less bothersome than the incredibly long wait. They left the waiting room and headed home, having decided to live with their afflictions rather than loitering interminably.

Other patients refused to leave and also refused the offers of reading materials and cleaning aids. They demanded to see the wizard immediately. They complained about the wait and grumbled about their neurotic symptoms to one another. They remain there still. Every once in a while, a staff member informs them they must wait a little longer and offers them a broom.

Constructive-Living Variations on Children's Story Themes

Can you find constructive-living meaning in the common fairy tales and Mother Goose rhymes listed below?

1. Red Riding Hood's fear of wolves; cause and treatment of a reality-based affliction.
2. Miss Muffett's spider phobia and how she overcame it.
3. Jack Horner acted on reality and discovered a plum! Getting at the truth.
4. Jack Spratt's cholesterol problem exacerbated by his wife's bulemia.
5. Georgie Porgie's flight from the boys and how he defeated his cowardice.
6. Little Boy Blue escaped from his responsibilities through sleep. What does he need to wake himself?
7. Old King Cole tried to show a merry face to everyone. He used his behavior and resources to keep up the charade. He needed to acknowledge and accept the sad moments, too.
8. Mary Mary was quite a cranky little girl. That's all right. What does she need to do?

9. Jack and Jill fell down. Now, pick up that pail and continue up the hill for water.
10. Reality brought that old woman who lived in the shoe a confined environment.
11. Old Mother Hubbard didn't have it so easy, either. Her dog needs to look elsewhere for a bone, and Mrs. Hubbard needs a job or Social Security.
12. Mary's lamb was a dependent clinging vine. What does the lamb need to do? How can Mary help?
13. Tom, the piper's son, did something wrong and paid the price. Or did he? What about restitution for the lost pig?
14. Jack is nimble, flexible. Even through the flame of adversity Jack can jump toward his goals.
15. Peter, the pumpkin eater, had marriage trouble. His solution was to restrict his wife. What did that do to his wife? What did it do to Peter?

References

Brandon, David. *Zen in the Art of Helping.* New York: Dell, 1976.

Fujita, Chihiro. *Morita Therapy.* New York, Tokyo: Igaku-shoin, 1986.

Huber, Jack. *Through an Eastern Window.* Boston: Houghton Mifflin, 1965.

Hyde, Lewis. *The Gift.* New York: Vintage, 1979.

Ishiyama, F. I. "A Case of Severe Test Anxiety Treated in Morita Therapy: Acceptance and Not Fighting It." *Canadian Counsellor* 17, 172–174, 1983.

Ishiyama, F. I. "Shyness: Anxious Social Sensitivity and Self Isolating Tendency." *Adolescence* 19, 903–911, 1984.

Ishiyama, F. I. "Brief Morita Therapy on Social Anxiety: A Single Case Study of Therapeutic Changes." *Canadian Journal of Counselling* 20, 56–65, 1986a.

Ishiyama, F. I. "Morita Therapy: Its Basic Features and Cognitive Intervention for Anxiety Treatment." *Psychotherapy* 23, 375–381, 1986b.

Ishiyama, F. I. "Positive Reinterpretation of Fear of Death: A Japanese (Morita) Psychotherapy Approach to Anxiety Treatment." *Psychotherapy* 23, 556–562, 1986c.

Ishiyama, F. Ishu. "Use of Morita Therapy in Shyness Counseling in the West: Promoting Clients' Self-Acceptance and Action Taking." *Journal of Counseling and Development* 65, 547–551, 1987.

Ishiyama, F. Ishu. "Current Status of Morita Therapy Research." *International Bulletin of Morita Therapy* 1, 58–83, 1988.

Kapleau, Philip. *The Three Pillars of Zen.* Tokyo: Weatherhill, 1965.

Kennett, Jiyu. *Selling Water by the River.* New York: Random House, 1972.

Kondo, Akihisa. "Morita Therapy: A Japanese Therapy for Neurosis." *American Journal of Psychoanalysis* 13, 31–37, 1953.
Kora, Takehisa, and Ohara, Kenshiro. "Morita Therapy." *Psychology Today* 6(10), 63–68, 1973.
Laing, R. D. *The Divided Self.* New York: Pantheon, 1969.
Leggett, Trevor. *Zen and the Ways.* Boulder: Shambhala, 1978.
Maezumi, Hakuyu, and Glassman, Bernard. *On Zen Practice.* Los Angeles: Zen Center, 1976.
McGee, Richard K. Review. *Contemporary Psychology* 31(10) 750–751, 1986.
Mills, C. W. "Situated Actions and Vocabularies of Motive." *American Sociological Review* 5, 904–915, 1940.
Mitchell, Stephen, ed. *Dropping Ashes on the Buddha: The Teaching of Zen Master Seung Sahn.* New York: Grove, 1976.
Morita, Masatake. *Seishin Ryoho Kogi.* Tokyo: Hakuyosha, 1983.
Morita, Masatake, and Mizutani, Keiji. *Jikaku to Satori he no Michi.* Tokyo: Hakuyosha, 1959.
Reynolds, David K. *Morita Psychotherapy.* (English, Japanese, and Spanish editions) Berkeley: University of California Press, 1976a.
Reynolds, David K. *Naikan Psychotherapy.* Chicago: University of Chicago, 1983.
Reynolds, David K. *The Quiet Therapies.* Honolulu: University Press of Hawaii, 1980.
Reynolds, David K. "Morita Psychotherapy." In *Handbook of Innovative Psychotherapies,* ed. R. Corsini, pp. 489–501. New York: Wiley, 1981.
Reynolds, David K. "Naikan Psychotherapy." In *Handbook of Innovative Psychotherapies,* ed. R. Corsini, pp. 544–553. New York: Wiley, 1981.
Reynolds, David K. "Psychocultural Perspectives on Death." In *Living and Dying with Cancer,* ed. P. Ahmed. New York: Elsevier, 1981.
Reynolds, David K. *Constructive Living.* Honolulu: University of Hawaii Press, 1984.
Reynolds, David K. *Playing Ball on Running Water.* New York: William Morrow, 1984.
Reynolds, David K. *Even in Summer the Ice Doesn't Melt.* New York: William Morrow, 1986.
Reynolds, David K. *Water Bears No Scars.* New York: William Morrow, 1987.
Reynolds, David K. *Pools of Lodging for the Moon.* New York: William Morrow, 1988.
Reynolds, David K. *A Thousand Waves.* New York: William Morrow, 1990.
Shibayama, Zenkei. *A Flower Does Not Talk.* Tokyo: Tuttle, 1970.
Suzuki, Daisetz. *The Training of the Zen Buddhist Monk.* New York: University Books, 1965.
Suzuki, Tomonori and Suzuki, Ryu. Morita Therapy. In *Psychosomatic*

Medicine, eds. Eric D. Wittkower and Hector Warnes, pp. 180–189. New York: Harper and Row, 1977.

Szasz, Thomas S. *The Myth of Mental Illness.* New York: Harper & Row, 1974.

Trungpa, Chogyam. *Cutting Through Spiritual Materialism.* Berkeley: Shambhala, 1973.

Wilber, Ken. *No Boundary.* Boulder: Shambala, 1981.

Wilson, William, transl. *Hagakure.* New York: Kodansha International, 1979.

Wood, Garth. *The Myth of Neurosis.* New York: Harper & Row, 1983.

REFERENCES

Information

For information about the nearest Constructive-Living instruction and Constructive-Living group programs call:

New York	(914) 255-3918
New York City	(212) 472-7925
Washington, D.C.	(703) 892-4174
Los Angeles	(213) 389-4088
Chicago	(708) 234-9394
Cleveland	(216) 321-0442

or contact Dr. Reynolds:
Constructive Living
P.O. Box 85
Coos Bay, Oregon 97420
(513) 269-5591

About the Author

David K. Reynolds, Ph.D., has been on the faculty of UCLA, the University of Southern California School of Medicine, and the University of Houston. He has written more than twenty books published in the United States and in Japan.

Recognized as the leading Western authority on Japanese psychotherapies, his work takes him around the United States in summer and to Japan each spring and fall. In 1988, at the invitation of the World Health Organization, Dr. Reynolds conducted Constructive Living training sessions for psychiatrists in the People's Republic of China. Currently he has a private practice in Constructive Living in Coos Bay, Oregon.